Organizational Digital Transformation

An IT-Enabled Program Approach

Organizational Digital Transformation

An IT-Enabled Program Approach

James J. Jiang, Gary Klein, and Judy Y. H. Huang

BEP

BUSINESS EXPERT PRESS

Leader in applied, concise business books

Organizational Digital Transformation:
An IT-Enabled Program Approach

Copyright © Business Expert Press, LLC, 2026.

Cover design by Cassandra Kronstedt

Interior design by S4Carlisle Publishing Services, Chennai, India

First published in 2025 by
Business Expert Press, LLC
222 East 46th Street, New York, NY 10017
www.businessexpertpress.com

ISBN-13: 978-1-63742-912-9 (paperback)
ISBN-13: 978-1-63742-913-6 (e-book)

Portfolio and Project Management Collection

First edition: 2025

10 9 8 7 6 5 4 3 2 1

EU SAFETY REPRESENTATIVE
Mare Nostrum Group B.V.
Mauritskade 21D
1091 GC Amsterdam
The Netherlands
gpsr@mare-nostrum.co.uk

Description

Digital transformation is a pivotal strategy for modern enterprises to enhance competitiveness and address rapidly changing market demands, encompassing comprehensive changes in business processes, business models, and organizational culture. To effectively achieve digital transformation, enterprises must leverage program management to coordinate multiple interdependent digital projects, thereby attaining overall benefits. Implementing digital transformation requires a well-managed program. To that end, we discuss the entire program management life cycle, encompassing the identification and establishment of programs, definition and planning of programs, execution and delivery of programs, and program closure. Each life cycle phase requires specific management activities and tools, many of which are described in this book, such as program vision statements, blueprints, and benefit realization management.

This book combines practical management theories and methods with case examples. It provides reference materials and practical tools for IT directors, C-suite executives, and business and IT professionals seeking to drive digital transformation. Chapters outline actionable steps for each program life cycle phase and provide practical tools, frameworks, and methodologies to guide readers in successfully managing digital transformation programs, ultimately achieving long-term success and sustainable development for their enterprises. Through an in-depth analysis of a virtual case, "Digital Transformation of *The Sun News*," readers will gain a deeper understanding and be able to apply the program management methodology and tools introduced in the book, which contribute to successful digital transformation initiatives.

This book is a valuable resource for business leaders, IT executives, and professionals pursuing digital transformation. The authors demonstrate the role of IT program management in aligning IT projects with business goals through practical frameworks and real-world insight. Contains include actionable templates and case studies to help organizations navigate digital transformation successfully and achieve long-term success.

Contents

List of Figures and Tables ix

Review Quotes xiii

Introduction xv

Chapter 1   Digital Transformation and IT-Enabled Program
Management 1

Chapter 2   Identifying and Formulating the Program 35

Chapter 3   Defining and Planning the Program 71

Chapter 4   Executing and Delivering the Program 101

Chapter 5   Closing the Program 129

Chapter 6   Conclusion 137

Glossary 165

About the Authors 169

Index 171

List of Figures and Tables

Figures

Figure I.1   The role of the project xvii

Figure I.2   The four types of projects within an organization xviii

Figure 1.1   Schematic diagram of an enterprise digital transformation program 4

Figure 1.2   Schematic diagram of two paths for digital strategy execution..6

Figure 1.3   IT-enabled program life cycle 9

Figure 1.4   Organizational level control diagram of digital transformation program 15

Figure 2.1   Main tasks of identifying and formulating programs 36

Figure 2.2   The Sun News's Organizational Strategy Map example....42

Figure 2.3   Stakeholder power and interest matrix............................45

Figure 2.4   Power and interest matrix example of *The Sun News*........49

Figure 2.5   The Program Strategy Map example of *The Sun News*'s digital integration program...................................53

Figure 3.1   Defining and planning the program 72

Figure 3.2   Program Business Case relationship chart.......................72

Figure 3.3   Program Business Case Planning Process........................74

Figure 3.4   *The Sun News*'s digital integration Program Blueprint example...76

Figure 3.5   Program benefits realization framework..........................78

Figure 3.6   Program benefits planning framework.............................78

Figure 3.7   Pathway to benefits and program objectives 79

Figure 3.8   Benefit Map example for *The Sun News* digital integration program 81

Figure 3.9   Completed Benefit Map for *The Sun News* digital integration program 84

Figure 3.10   The Benefit Dependence Map for *The Sun News* digital integration program...86

Figure 3.11   Project Dossier for *The Sun News* digital integration
program 88

Figure 3.12   Program organizational structure diagram 95

Figure 4.1   Program execution and delivery...................................102

Figure 4.2   Benefit delivery life cycle 103

Figure 4.3   Benefit Map example for *The Sun News* digital
integration program 106

Figure 4.4   Revised Program Benefit Map 107

Figure 4.5   Program benefits realization trend chart (first year
of execution for *The Sun News*'s digital integration
program) 110

Figure 4.6   Benefits achievement status one year after *The Sun
News*'s digital integration program..............................111

Figure 4.7   Program benefits realization trend chart (second
year of execution for *The Sun News*'s digital
integration program) 112

Figure 4.8   Program benefits realization trend chart (third year
of execution for *The Sun News*'s digital integration
program) 112

Figure 4.9   Benefits achievement status two years after the
execution of *The Sun News*'s digital integration
program 113

Figure 4.10   Benefits achievement status three years after the
execution of *The Sun News*'s digital integration
program 114

Figure 4.11   Characteristics of VUCA..116

Figure 4.12   Revised Program Benefits Dependency Map 119

Figure 4.13   Revised Program Benefits Dependency Map
based on requirements..125

Figure 5.1   Program closure activities 129

Figure 6.1   Cultural and technological dimensions of IT-enabled
program management 140

Figure 6.2   Organizational strategy drives projects..........................144

Figure 6.3   IT program driving organizational strategic change.......147

Figure 6.4   Digital transformation strategy implementation
model...147

Tables

Table I.1   Summary of differences in project management
approaches xx

Table I.2   The three types of program management...................... xxii

Table 2.1   Pre-program activities example for *The Sun News*'s
digital integration program..40

Table 2.2   Program Stakeholder Map.................................43

Table 2.3   Stakeholder Map example for *The Sun News* digital
transformation 44

Table 2.4   Stakeholder Profile example for *The Sun News*.................47

Table 2.5   *The Sun News*'s digital integration program
vision example..49

Table 2.6   The Program Mandate of *The Sun News*'s digital
integration program 54

Table 2.7   The Program Brief of *The Sun News* digital
integration program 58

Table 2.8   The Program Preparation Plan of *The Sun News*
digital integration program............................63

Table 3.1   Current state and future state of *The Sun News* case
example...75

Table 3.2   Benefits Profile example of *The Sun News* digital
integration program 83

Table 3.3   Project Dossier example for *The Sun News* digital
integration program 89

Table 3.4   Program Governance Plan example for *The Sun News*
digital integration program............................92

Table 4.1   Benefits measurement indicators and performance
metrics in the Program Benefit Profile...........................108

Table 4.2   The revised Project Dossier of *The Sun News* digital
integration program 121

Table 6.1   Alignment of program management practices with
change management stages.............................143

Review Quotes

"*Over the years, I have read countless books on digital transformation and project management, but* Organizational Digital Transformation: An IT-Enabled Program Approach *is one of the very few practical books that fully integrates a strategic vision with execution tools and truly brings them to life. This book's interpretation of digital transformation goes far beyond superficial slogans; it uses a rigorous logical framework to systematically explain how to translate a transformation blueprint into measurable results through IT-enabled program management—covering everything from strategy formulation and program design to benefits realization. If you are a senior IT executive, an IT manager at any level, a digital transformation program manager, or a core member of a PMO team, this book will become the most essential guide in your toolbox. It not only helps us identify risks and blind spots along the transformation journey but also provides an evidence-based action framework to assist you in making the right decisions in complex and dynamic environments. This is a professional classic worth reading, verifying, and practicing repeatedly. I sincerely recommend it to all leaders at the forefront of IT-enabled organizational transformation.*"—**Michael Kung, Sr. Executive Partner, Executive Programs, Gartner**

"*This book cuts through the clutter to give educators and leaders a sharp, practical playbook for guiding big change. Richly illustrated with real-world examples and equipped with tools aligned to industry best practices, it's built for teaching and doing both, without the heavy-textbook feel. This concise, executive-style guide serves as a key to success, whether you are developing a course or spearheading a transformation, enabling you to seamlessly integrate theory and practice.*"—**Dr. Jacob Chia-An Tsai, Department of Information Management, National Central University, Taiwan**

"The book delivers an exceptional level of professionalism and depth. For newcomers or practitioners seeking to transition from project to program, or from tactical execution to strategic delivery, this book serves as a rare and valuable roadmap. The author's description of the program manager's role is particularly well articulated, emphasizing a critical truth: The success of a program manager is not defined by whether individual projects are completed, but by whether the intended strategy is realized. A great program manager is not merely an executor of strategy but a strategic interpreter and real-time navigator. In this context, this book is undoubtedly an outstanding work in the field of IT program management."—**Raymond Chang, Executive Vice President, Digital, Data & Technology Department, KGI Financial**

Introduction

In today's rapidly changing business environment, organizations require a clear mission and objectives to guide development. A mission represents the fundamental purpose of an organization's existence. For instance, the mission of the media industry is to provide quality news information and promote social progress. This mission aims to achieve comprehensive societal development by reporting facts, disseminating knowledge, and inspiring discussion, thus enhancing civic quality and maintaining social justice. Such missions reflect the significant role and responsibilities of the media in society, demanding that it remains independent, impartial, and objective in its reporting to earn public trust.

Based on their mission, organizations establish corresponding objectives. Organizational objectives encapsulate the mission and serve as short- and mid-term plans to achieve long-term visions. To continue the media example, the objectives of its mission may include enhancing public knowledge, promoting civic engagement, strengthening social oversight, and driving policy reforms.

To achieve these objectives, organizations formulate strategies and tactics as a means to reach their goals. For example, media organizations might adopt the following strategies: expanding news coverage to ensure the presentation of diverse perspectives, investing in digital transformation to enhance the user experience on online news platforms, and organizing public forums and lectures to facilitate exchange and discussion among various sectors of society. Specific tactics could include establishing specialized reporting teams to thoroughly investigate major news events, developing news applications that provide real-time news updates and personalized recommendations, and collaborating with other media outlets, academic institutions, and nongovernmental organizations to enhance the professionalism and authority of their reporting. These strategies and tactics aim to strengthen public trust and reliance on the media by providing high-quality news content and services, thus fulfilling their mission and objectives.

These organizational strategies and tactics are not achieved overnight; they are realized through a series of concrete projects and initiatives. For instance, a media organization may launch a news website, establish a section for special reports, host forums, and plan large-scale public events as part of its strategy. Each project is a crucial component in realizing the organization's strategy, and successful project execution propels the achievement of the mission. Moreover, the projects enhance the organization's innovation capabilities and competitiveness, helping it stand out in an increasingly competitive market. For example, launching a news website can attract a different audience, establishing a special report section can improve the depth and quality of reporting, and hosting forums and public events can increase the organization's social influence and public engagement.

Once project deliverables are handed over to operational units, they become part of the organization's daily operations. For example, regularly updating the news website's content, continuously hosting high-quality public forums, and optimizing reporting content and formats based on audience feedback. These operational activities require ongoing investment and management to ensure long-term stable operation and continuous generation of expected benefits. For instance, updating news website content requires a professional editorial team and technical support; hosting high-quality public forums necessitates meticulous planning and organization; and optimizing content requires constant data analysis and audience surveys. These operational activities ensure the achievement of organizational strategies and objectives, contributing to the organization's sustained brand value and market influence.

Organizations can achieve their mission and objectives through such strategies and projects, maintaining a leading position in an increasingly competitive business environment and bringing more positive benefits and impact. In summary, projects play a crucial role in executing organizational strategies. They are not only for completing specific tasks but also key avenues for advancing the execution of organizational strategies and achieving long-term goals (as illustrated in Figure I.1). Projects are the mechanism to convert the mission, objectives, strategies, and tactics into operations that capitalize on the marketplace.

Figure I.1 The role of the project

Projects within an organization exist in four circumstances described by Vuorinen and Martinsuo as illustrated in Figure I.2 (full source identified in the complementary readings list at the end of the introduction). Management of a Project Network (left lower quadrant) involves a single project that spans multiple organizations. An example is the collaboration of several technology companies to develop a new technology platform. In such cases, each participating organization is responsible for a portion of the project, requiring high levels of coordination and communication to ensure the project's overall success. Such communication involves cross-organizational agreements and contract management to ensure all parties agree on responsibilities, resource sharing, timelines, and other factors.

When multiple projects involving multiple organizations are managed, it is referred to as Management of a Business Network (right lower quadrant in Figure I.2). For instance, an automobile manufacturer working with part suppliers and logistics companies aims to optimize the entire supply chain process to enhance efficiency and reduce costs. This improvement requires close cooperation in technical integration (such as

Multiple projects

- **Objective:** To make *projects* as tools for creating business value

- **Approach:** Managing multiple projects within an organization to implement the business strategy

Single project

Multiple projects in a firm
"Management of project business"

Example: IT-enabled transformation program or digital investment portfolio

Multiple projects across multiple firms
"Management of a business network"

Example: Supply chain optimization project or public infrastructure project

A project in a firm
"Management of a project"

Example: Product development project or IT project

A project across multiple firms
"Management of a project network"

Example: Digital platform development project or construction project

Intrafirm

Interfirms

Figure I.2 *The four types of projects within an organization*

sharing precise technical specifications and designs between the manufacturer and parts suppliers), quality standards (negotiating and establishing strict quality control processes), delivery schedules (coordinating to avoid supply chain disruptions), and cost control (negotiating favorable supply terms, optimizing production processes, and improving transportation efficiency). This complex class of projects requires coordinating resources, policies, and interests across multiple enterprises and organizations, involving multilayered management and oversight. This management approach emphasizes systematic thinking and overall synergy to achieve common goals.

Managing a single project within a single organization is termed Management of a Project (left upper quadrant of Figure I.2). For example, developing a new product within a company will typically have clear objectives, timelines, and resource allocations, with a Project Manager overseeing all aspects from inception to completion, including planning, execution, monitoring, and closure.

Managing many related projects within a single organization that executes the same strategy is known as the Management of Project Business (right upper quadrant of Figure I.2). The primary aim of this project class is to achieve strategic goals and benefits (such as enhancing market competitiveness, increasing customer satisfaction, and expanding market share) and creating value (boosting revenue, reducing costs, and enhancing brand value). Integration and coordination are key in project business management, where each project operates independently but contributes to the same strategic goal. For example, an organization's digital transformation strategy to enhance competitiveness and business efficiency involves multiple related projects. Appropriate project management ensures that a group of related projects operates cohesively, with rational resource allocation, strict progress control, and effective risk management. As in the case of digitally transforming traditional print media, the strategy includes developing new digital platforms, enhancing user experience on existing websites, utilizing big data analysis to optimize content for the audience, training employees to adapt to digital workflows, and several other initiatives. Effective project management methods are essential for organizations to achieve their strategic objectives and enhance overall operational efficiency.

Table I.1 Summary of differences in project management approaches

	Portfolio management	Project management	Program management
Definition	Ensuring projects align with corporate strategic goals through project evaluation and portfolio optimization to maximize corporate returns.	Planning, executing, and controlling a single project.	Govern and integrate related projects and other activities to achieve expected business benefits and create stakeholder value.
Objective	Choosing the optimal project investment portfolio under limited resources.	Focus on delivering specific project outcomes, such as developing a new product or service.	Focus on implementing overall organizational strategic and benefit goals.
Scope	All projects and programs for a broadly specified context (often the entire organization).	Single project.	Encompasses multiple related projects, often spanning different teams and departments.
Role	The Portfolio Manager communicates with executive-level portfolio governance on how portfolio components align with strategic goals.	The Project Manager is responsible for planning and executing a single project.	The Program Manager coordinates multiple projects to ensure they align with organizational goals. The Business Change Manager ensures the program delivers benefits to operations.
Focus	Selecting and supporting multiple projects or programs guided by available resources and corporate strategic plans.	Focus on project details and deliverables.	Focus on overall program progress, coordination, risk, and resource allocation.
Facing change	Track changes.	Avoid changes.	Adapt to changes.

For managing projects within a single organization, we summarize three project management methods—Portfolio Management, Project Management, and Program Management—based on information from project management sources and academic articles. Table I.1 presents the distinct differences among these three methods.

Significant differences exist among project, portfolio, and program management, yet they all share the common goal of achieving organizational strategic objectives. Portfolio management involves selecting the appropriate programs and projects, providing the necessary resources, and prioritizing tasks. For example, within a technology company, a portfolio management process evaluates and selects multiple research and development projects, such as AI research, Internet-of-Things (IoT) platform development, and blockchain application development, ensuring reasonable resource allocation and prioritizing key projects based on market demands and organizational strategy.

On the other hand, project management focuses on accomplishing the defined project deliverables through planning and execution, thereby achieving subgoals or subcomponents within programs or portfolios and contributing to the realization of organizational strategic objectives. For instance, the management of a new product development project must ensure that each phase proceeds as planned and is completed within budget and time constraints, thereby supporting the success of the entire product line.

Program management involves coordinating the projects, resources, and stakeholders, as well as managing the interdependencies among these elements to achieve the intended benefits. For example, when a company implements an omnichannel marketing strategy, this may include multiple interrelated projects such as upgrading e-commerce platforms, social media marketing systems, and customer data integration. In this omnichannel marketing strategy, program management must coordinate the progress and resources of each project, ensure seamless data exchange and collaboration between the e-commerce platform, social media marketing system, and customer data platform, manage the interdependencies among these projects, and ensure each project is executed as planned to achieve the expected benefits, ultimately realizing the overall goal of the omnichannel marketing strategy (e.g., increasing sales or enhancing brand awareness).

Increasingly, managers recognize the appropriateness of program management when executing strategies aimed at achieving benefits and creating value. This recognition stems from the fact that managing all related projects under a single strategy in an integrated manner can yield

Table I.2 The three types of program management

Typology	Compliance	Emergent	Vision-led
Reason for Formation	Formed due to organizational pressure from legal or market forces.	Formed when potential sponsors identify that integrating specific initiated projects with common goals or relevance will yield greater benefits.	Constructed based on strategic objectives.
Key to Success	Plans that must be executed.	Identifying interdependencies among projects through integration, developing common strategies to minimize negative business impacts, and focusing on business benefits rather than simple outputs.	Adopting an organic organizational structure that can flexibly adapt to environmental changes, granting employees higher autonomy to focus on innovation.
Program Leader's Role	Ensuring regulatory requirements are clearly understood, assigning responsibilities to project teams, monitoring adherence to legal or policy standards, reporting progress to senior management, and coordinating efforts to meet compliance deadlines.	Identifying clear vision and needs, formulating common strategies, selecting and integrating projects for execution, and reviewing and reallocating projects.	Developing business plans, clarifying the team's vision, linking organizational planning changes, integrating cooperation among units, and managing stakeholders effectively.

overall benefits that are unattainable through individual project management. This integrated management approach enhances resource utilization efficiency, reduces redundancy, and ensures project synergies. Based on the initiation process, programs can be categorized into three types: compliance, emergent, and vision-led (as shown in Table I.2).

Compliance programs are formed due to organizational pressure from legal or market forces and are known as must-execute programs. The Program Leader in such initiatives plays a focused and directive role, centered on ensuring that compliance objectives are met efficiently and accurately. This practice involves ensuring that regulatory requirements are clearly understood and effectively translated into project-level activities, assigning specific responsibilities to relevant project teams, monitoring ongoing adherence to legal and policy standards, reporting compliance progress to senior management, and coordinating cross-functional efforts to meet regulatory deadlines. For example, a company may launch multiple related projects to comply with new environmental regulations, such as upgrading production equipment to reduce carbon emissions, implementing renewable energy systems, and training employees on new environmental standards. Although these initiatives share similarities with broader program types, the leader's role is largely operational, emphasizing timely and correct execution rather than strategic or emergent innovation.

Emergent programs coordinate existing but previously uncoordinated projects to achieve necessary changes and benefits. These programs are formed when potential sponsors recognize that integrating ongoing projects or activities under unified management will yield greater benefits. For instance, a large retail company facing market competition pressures might simultaneously initiate projects to upgrade its online shopping platform, optimize its logistics system, and improve customer service. Although these projects were initially conducted independently, management may find that integrating them under a single program allows for more effective resource allocation, reduced implementation time, and enhanced overall competitiveness, thereby opting to manage them collectively.

This book focuses on *vision-led programs*, the most mature type of program. These programs often have clearly defined visions or desired change objectives and are constructed based on strategic goals. For example, an organization might establish multiple projects to improve efficiency, including the application (or development) of new technologies, market expansion, and professional talent training. Such programs pursue technological innovation, focusing on market expansion and talent development to ensure the organization enhances efficiency and maintains competitiveness in a rapidly changing environment. Vision-led programs are characterized by complexity and ambiguity. Digital transformation programs, for instance, are initiated based on the organization's top-level goals but involve long execution periods and rapidly changing technological issues. During the various phases of the program management life cycle, sponsors may halt the program or make significant changes.

Therefore, this book delves into the program management life cycle, combining real-life cases and management theories to provide managers with practical tools and methods for effective program management. By following the examples and guidance in this book, readers can gain a deeper understanding of and better manage digital transformation programs, ultimately achieving long-term success and sustainable development for their organizations. Through an in-depth exploration of program management, managers can learn how to tackle complex and rapidly evolving technological issues and apply program management tools flexibly to achieve optimal strategic outcomes.

Features of This Book

Use of Case Studies

This book uses a fictional case study, "Digital Transformation of *The Sun News*," as a practical example to help readers better understand the concepts of IT-enabled program management, the tools for IT-enabled program management, and how companies manage digital transformation programs from start to finish. We assume *The Sun News* undertook a significant digital transformation, successfully transitioning from a traditional print media outlet to a digital media company embracing new technologies. *The Sun News* continues to deepen its application of digital technology in its news media operations. Although *The Sun News*'s digital transformation is ongoing, from a program life cycle perspective, the company has completed several large-scale transformation projects. *The Sun News*'s IT-enabled program, aimed at digital integration, serves as a practical case to introduce management tools for the four governance phases of IT-enabled programs. By illustrating *The Sun News*'s successful digital transformation, readers can gain a better understanding of the four IT-enabled program management governance phases and the necessary management tools for each phase. Furthermore, *The Sun News*'s digital transformation integrates the three key aspects of digital transformation listed earlier (business process transformation, business model transformation, and organizational/cultural transformation). The case study will explore *The Sun News*'s digital transformation journey from inception to the significant milestone of achieving its digital integration goals.

Book Structure

The chapters of this book are organized according to the phases of the program management life cycle, preceded by a comprehensive introduction to program management and followed by a concluding discussion on culture, technology, and change management. Each chapter has case examples and a suggested list of complementary readings (which include citation information for references to outside material). The objectives of each chapter are as follows.

Chapter 1—Digital Transformation and IT-Enabled Program Management: This chapter explains why digital transformation requires a program management approach, briefly describes the four stages of the program life cycle, and outlines the Program Manager's three primary responsibilities and five core skills.

Chapter 2—Identifying and Formulating the Program: This chapter explains the main activities involved in identifying and formulating a program, including producing a Program Mandate, a Program Brief, and a Program Preparation Plan for the next phase.

Chapter 3—Defining and Planning the Program: This chapter describes the main activities for defining and planning a program, including producing a Program Business Case and a detailed execution plan for moving to the next phase.

Chapter 4—Executing and Delivering the Program: This chapter details the main activities of executing and delivering a program, including benefit realization management, implementing control methods, and continuous stakeholder communication to ensure alignment with organizational goals.

Chapter 5—Closing the Program: This chapter discusses the timing for closing a program, formally ending the program to allow team members to return to their operational departments, and ensuring a proper transition to maintain the realized benefits.

Chapter 6—Conclusion: This chapter discusses the culture–technology view in the IT-enabled program management process and further introduces a digital transformation program case to present the linkage between change management and IT-enabled program management.

While each chapter of this book contributes to a broad understanding of IT-enabled program management, readers may benefit from focusing on specific parts depending on their professional roles. Chapters 1, 2, and 6 emphasize the formation, definition, and strategic implications of digital transformation programs. These chapters are especially relevant for C-suite executives, as they provide critical insights into vision-setting, strategic alignment, and cultural shifts that drive successful transformation initiatives.

Chapters 3 to 5, on the other hand, concentrate on the execution, delivery, and closure phases of IT-enabled programs. These chapters provide practical tools and detailed management methods essential for Program Managers and implementation leaders responsible for operationalizing strategic initiatives and ensuring the realization of benefits.

That said, all chapters are interconnected and essential to the overall narrative. For any organization seeking to adopt IT program management tools to implement a digital transformation strategy, the integrated knowledge presented offers guidance across roles and responsibilities. Anyone engaged in IT-enabled organizational transformation—whether from a strategic or implementation perspective—should develop an understanding of the whole program life cycle but may selectively pursue key tools specific to their positions.

Complementary Reading

Jiang, J., G. Klein, and W. Huang. 2020. *Projects, Programs, and Portfolios in Strategic Organizational Transformation.* Business Expert Press.
Vuorinen, L., and M. Martinsuo, eds. 2024. "Introduction to Management of Project Business." In *Management of Project Business.* Tampere University.

CHAPTER 1

Digital Transformation and IT-Enabled Program Management

Digital Transformation

Today's businesses are undergoing rapid transformation, driven by increased competition and rising customer expectations. Digital transformation is a crucial component of an overall business transformation strategy and a key factor in determining the success or failure of such efforts. Combining the right technologies, personnel, processes, and operations can enhance an organization's ability to respond quickly to disruptions, seize opportunities, and meet customers' evolving needs while simultaneously driving future growth and innovation in unexpected ways. Digital transformation involves leveraging digital technologies and artificial intelligence to fundamentally change an organization's operational processes and business models, enabling it to adapt to the ever-changing market and customer demands. It encompasses comprehensive organizational change, prompting businesses to rethink their technology investments, personnel, and processes to fully transform their operating models, value propositions, and customer experiences, thereby creating new value for the enterprise.

Digital transformation can be divided into three stages: Digitalization, Digital Optimization, and Digital Transformation. Digitalization describes how IT or digital technologies change business processes. Cloud management and the Internet-of-Things are examples of digitalization. After digitalization, companies become familiar with digital tools, which further optimize and improve current operations and efficiency, or enhance customer satisfaction. Both digitalization and digital optimization can be seen as preparatory steps for digital transformation. To achieve digital transformation, a company must fundamentally overhaul its entire business strategy and processes. Introducing new digital technologies is crucial for driving digital transformation, which results in changes to business processes, business models, and organizational culture.

Digital transformation plans focus on the following three key areas:

Business Process Transformation: As a crucial component of business transformation, digital transformation primarily involves changing and adjusting core processes and workflows. The aim is to automate processes to meet evolving business objectives, competition, and customer demands. The technology framework established through this transformation closely relates to business processes, supporting and promoting process changes. With additional workflow optimization, business process performance can improve after the operations are completed. For instance, a company can reduce downtime, streamline production processes, and increase profitability by deploying a cloud-based supply chain management system.

Business Model Transformation: Unlike business process transformation, which focuses on workflows and tasks, business model transformation mainly addresses the fundamental components of value delivery in specific industries. For example, in the automotive industry, digital technology helps centralize and automate subscription-based business models and billing processes. With rapidly changing customer demands and cultural shifts, the traditional car purchasing procedure is gradually evolving into a subscription-based business model.

Organizational and Cultural Transformation: Successful digital transformation must align with organizational culture and values. If there is a lack of internal agreement on company culture, employee productivity, motivation, and overall well-being can be negatively impacted. The slow or reluctant adoption of emerging digital technologies can lead to unmet goals, ultimately harming a company's competitiveness, revenue, and brand value.

The above three aspects of digital transformation illustrate its broad impact on organizations. However, successful applications are rare, often resulting from poor planning, uncoordinated goals, and vague strategies. The primary task of digital transformation is to formulate a digital strategy and integrate it as a key component of the business development strategy. Then, the strategy must be thoroughly formulated and skillfully integrated into practice. Integration involves embedding data-driven concepts, methods, and mechanisms throughout the organization to align with its vision, goals, and business ecosystem blueprint proposed by its overall development strategy. A systematic design of a digital transformation strategy outlines the goals, directions, actions, and resource requirements essential for successful integration.

Strategic design implementation refers to aligning and coordinating internal resources (personnel, business processes, IT systems, funds) to achieve the goals set during the strategy formulation process, ensuring the ultimate strategic objectives are met. Key aspects of strategy implementation include resource organization, leadership structure, communication, incentives, and control mechanisms. The process of transitioning an organization from the strategic management phase (strategic activities) to the operational management phase (operational activities) is often referred to as strategy execution. Operational management refers to the day-to-day business activities within an organization, typically represented by various operational activities across different departments, such as logistics management activities in the logistics department or marketing management activities in the marketing department. For digital transformation, the proposed digital strategy, as a newly planned organizational strategic goal, often inherently conflicts with the current operational activities based on outdated strategic goals. Failing to bridge the gap between the digital strategy and current operational activities is a fundamental reason for digital strategy failure. Achieving successful digital strategy execution is facilitated through program management.

Program Management: The Bridge Between Digital Strategy and Digital Operations

Conducting digital transformation is fundamentally a program management issue. Scholars in the field of project management suggest that an organization's strategic change objectives are best organized and implemented through change programs. This suggestion implies that enterprises must coordinate and manage multiple interdependent change projects to achieve integrated benefits that cannot be obtained through single-project management, thereby realizing the organization's strategic change goals, including digital transformation.

Achieving an organization's digital transformation objectives through a single digital project would be too challenging. Instead, the transformation requires coordinated management of multiple digital projects. For instance, these projects may include employee digital skills training projects, the development, purchase, and deployment of digital infrastructure projects, and various digitalization projects for different business processes or segments, as shown in Figure 1.1. Companies may focus on different business processes depending on their priorities and objectives.

Due to the complex interdependencies among these projects, managing any single project in isolation while ignoring its related projects will not lead to successful digital transformation at the organizational level. Therefore, these projects must be viewed as a program and managed in a coordinated manner (as further illustrated in Figure 1.1). To distinguish this program, we refer to it as an IT-enabled program applied to implementing a digital strategy.

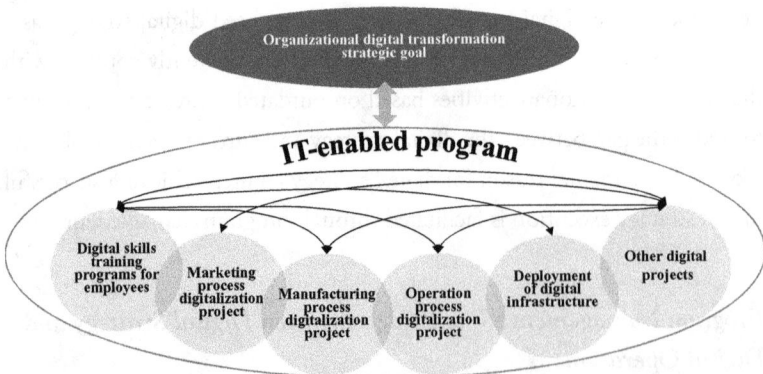

Figure 1.1 Schematic diagram of an enterprise digital transformation program

Program Management: Ensuring a Soft Landing for Digital Strategy

From a project management perspective, management scholars have noted that strategy implementation can be viewed as a distinct type of project or program. However, when managing the implementation of a digital strategy as a unique "project," it is essential to pay attention to the three following complexities.

Firstly, the digital transformation "project" is a multiproject management issue (as analyzed earlier). Secondly, the objectives of a digital transformation "project" are often ambiguous, and the solutions to achieve these objectives are uncertain. Digital transformation is characterized by high levels of uncertainty, encompassing environmental, technological, and organizational risks. Therefore, the digital strategy objectives set by many organizations are often growth-oriented and broadly interpretable, allowing for adjustments during the implementation process to ensure that the digital transformation truly creates benefits and value. The uncertainty of the objectives also implies uncertainty in the solutions, meaning that many enterprises finalize their digital transformation plans through a gradual exploration process. Lastly, there is a unique political aspect to digital transformation "projects." Being a strategic change, digital transformation inherently involves political maneuvering among internal stakeholders and vested interests. For digital transformation "projects," effectively balancing the conflicting interests of organizational stakeholders is crucial to the "project's success."

Since strategy forms the foundation for organizations to select projects, build programs, and allocate resources within these programs, it is vital to prioritize corporate strategy throughout the program management process. In program management, whether in program selection, resource allocation, project coordination, or project evaluation, the fundamental goal must always revolve around organizational strategy, making it the cornerstone of program management. The core task of program management is to align its initial goals with those of the organization and consistently maintain alignment with organizational strategic objectives throughout the program's life cycle.

Moreover, a program acts as a bridge between corporate strategy and operations, adapting to changes in strategy and operations. As shown in Figure 1.2, digital program management begins by embracing the

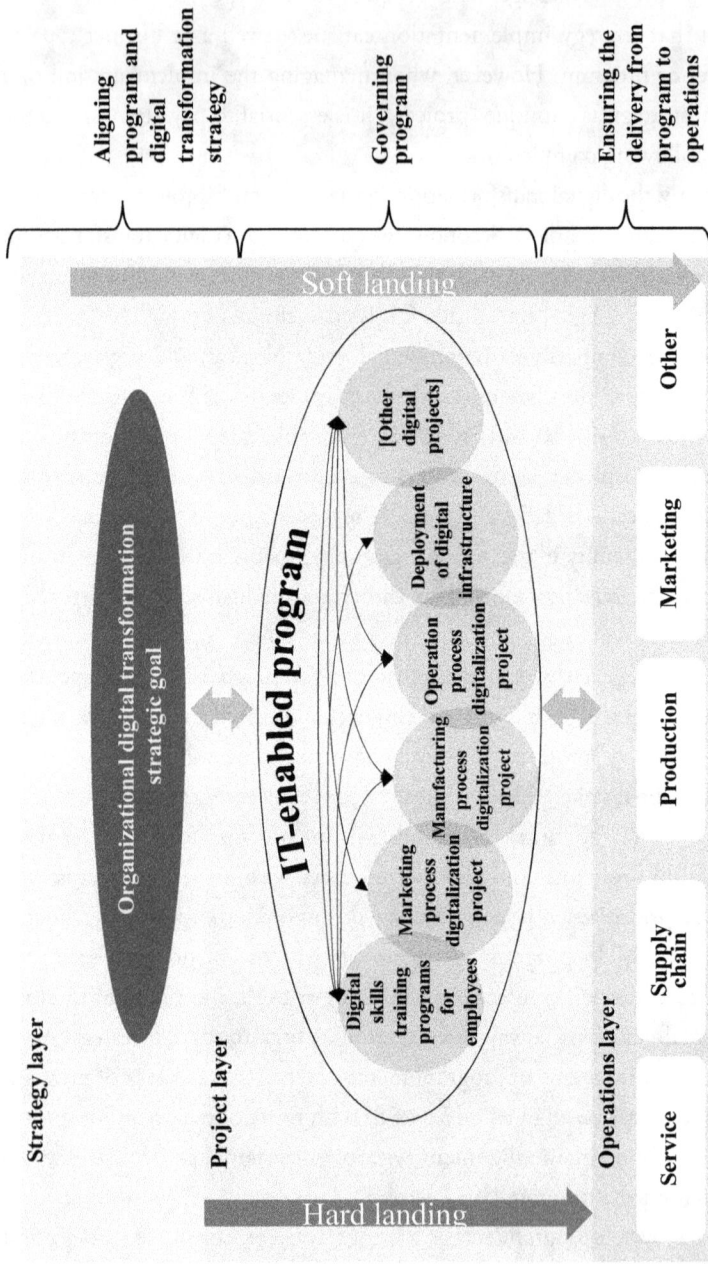

Figure 1.2 Schematic diagram of two paths for digital strategy execution

organization's digital strategic goals and gradually decomposing and translating these strategic objectives into various digital projects. The outcomes of these digital projects are then integrated and delivered at the operational level, thereby achieving digitalization at this level. A focus on the program without attention to the linkage from strategy to operations results in a hard landing of the program—an inability to realize the benefits of the capital and personnel resources spent. A soft landing occurs only when the program is firmly targeted at delivering operational changes aligned with evolving strategies.

If the digital strategic goals evolve, timely adjustments can be made by adding, deleting, or modifying digital projects within the IT-enabled program. This adjustment ensures that the final delivery of the IT-enabled program aligns with the ultimate digital strategic goals. Additionally, if there is feedback during the digitalization integration at the operational level, specific adjustments to the digital strategy can be made through the program's cyclical control mechanisms. This process demonstrates that the IT-enabled program, as a temporary organization, effectively bridges digital strategy and digital operations. The top-down strategy implementation and bottom-up feedback transmission minimize the misalignment and disconnect between strategy and operations. As a buffer zone, the IT-enabled program also mitigates the abrupt impact of strategic changes on the operational level, preventing a hard landing. In summary, a digital transformation program is an IT-enabled program executed simultaneously or sequentially, consisting of multiple interrelated digital and supporting projects or activities to achieve the transformation's strategic goals.

IT-Enabled Program Management

IT-enabled program management involves iterative processes that apply technology to drive action within the target organization for a set of related IT and supporting projects, delivering IT-based value to multiple stakeholders. In the process of IT-enabled program management, five key attributes require special attention, including the participating units or specific organizations, the scope of changes occurring within the organization, the interaction between IT and the organization, the adjustments made during different stages of the program life cycle, and the outcomes of IT-enabled program management.

Life Cycle of IT-Enabled Program Management: Four Phases

To successfully achieve digital transformation goals and expected benefits, enterprises must understand how to realize digital transformation through a series of interconnected, iterative steps. Figure 1.3 illustrates the life cycle of an IT-enabled program and the primary governance phases required for successful delivery. The external environment serves as a stimulus that prompts organizations to recognize the need for change. When technology begins to transform culture, society, and even nations, organizations must consider making adjustments to adapt and cope with the impacts, changes, and challenges brought about by the external environment. When organizations recognize the impact of technology on their operations, they must reconsider their IT and organizational strategies. Based on the expected goals of the organizational strategy, the IT-enabled program should be planned and executed to best support the organization's strategy.

Each phase of the life cycle may require multiple iterations, especially during the execution and delivery phase, where delivery capability and benefit realization are crucial, as IT-enabled programs deliver planned capabilities and benefits through multiple projects. The following introduces the four main governance phases in the life cycle of an IT-enabled program. The execution methods for each phase will be explained in detail in Chapters 2 through 5.

Phase 1—Identifying and Formulating an IT-Enabled Program: In phase 1, there are three major tasks: identifying the pre-program, formulating the program, and obtaining approval to proceed. Two governance themes in identifying the pre-program are strategic (value) decision management and stakeholder analysis, both of which play a foundational role in shaping the program's direction and ensuring alignment with organizational strategic goals. Strategic decision management concerns making clear and precise choices for an IT-enabled program among various strategic values (such as IT-based capabilities) to address factors triggering organizational change. These decisions help define the program's strategic intent and

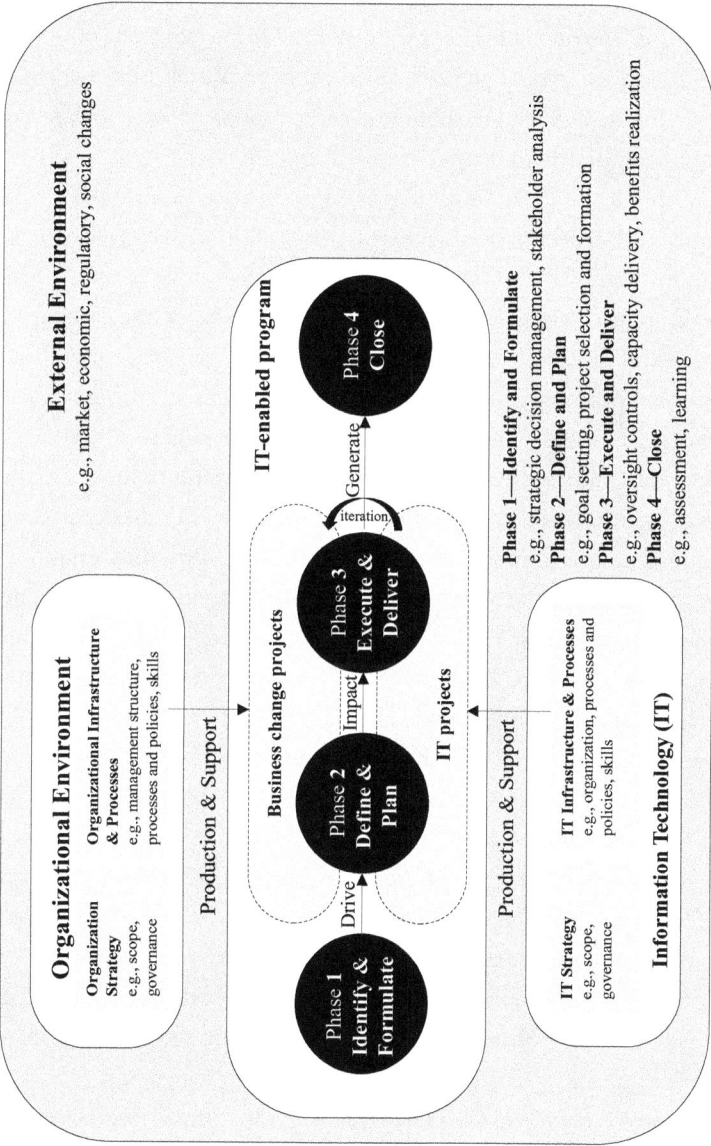

Figure 1.3 IT-enabled program life cycle

value proposition. By prioritizing strategic decision making at this stage, organizations ensure that the program is not only technically feasible but also strategically aligned with broader goals. The selection is based on the benefit–cost ratio of different options and the organization's readiness for each choice. The outcome of strategic decision management at this phase is typically presented as an IT-enabled program Vision Statement and a Program Brief, which are submitted for approval by the board, senior management, or other potential stakeholders.

Stakeholder analysis, on the other hand, focuses on considering the feedback and expected needs, benefits, and value perspectives of individuals or groups affected by or critical to the program's success. A quality stakeholder analysis conducted at the beginning of the IT-enabled program will determine whether the program will be approved and also identify any potential resistance that may arise in subsequent phases. Additionally, stakeholder input can help refine the program's vision, align expectations, and secure commitment across organizational levels. By embedding stakeholder analysis into the pre-program identification phase, organizations improve the program's social feasibility and long-term effectiveness. Collectively, these two governance themes in identifying pre-program ensure that the program is both strategically relevant and operationally supported. They form the basis for a program vision that is coherent, justifiable, and grounded in the organizational context, thereby increasing the likelihood of success throughout the program life cycle.

Phase 2—Defining and Planning IT-enabled Program: Once the Program Sponsor individual or group (typically one or more executives of the C-suite) approves the formulated IT-enabled program, the next phase is defining and planning the IT-enabled program. In phase 2, two major tasks need to be completed: developing the Program Business Case and obtaining approval to proceed. Three key governance themes that emerged during this phase are objective management, program documentation design, and organizational and personnel arrangements.

Objective management involves setting the overall program objectives and breaking them down into multiple project objectives. At this phase, it is recommended that higher program objectives be set and a consensus reached among the program management team (including the Program Manager and Project Managers). A key issue to address during objective management is the conflict between program-level objectives/needs and project-level objectives/needs.

There are two types of projects or activities in IT-enabled programs: business projects based on organizational infrastructure and processes and IT projects based on IT infrastructure and processes, as shown in Figure 1.3. After designing the program documentation to cover both types, the organization and structure of the IT-enabled program, as well as the personnel arrangements, should be determined. Important contingency measures will include the program environment and program characteristics. After planning the organization and structure, personnel arrangement plans, roles, and responsibilities will be formulated and documented. All planning documents will further progress through the life cycle.

Phase 3—Executing and Delivering IT-Enabled Program: The recently defined IT-enabled program and related planning will guide the execution phase of the program. The main governance themes for executing IT-enabled programs include monitoring, delivering IT capabilities, and realizing IT-based benefits. Additionally, governance at this phase is considered an iterative process. Monitoring and controlling the program during execution receives extensive academic attention. Governance mechanisms for IT-enabled programs include risk and resistance management, blueprinting, visioning, structural design, technical controls, and cultural control (also referred to as clan control). Observing and adequately managing the competition and coordination among internal projects within the IT-enabled program is key to success.

Delivered IT and business capabilities must be transformed into organizational operational capabilities to realize IT-based value or benefits. Managing this transformation may encounter resistance due to organizational inertia. Aligning deliverables with organizational functions and adapting to changing strategies is essential for realizing benefits. Finally, it is important to note that there is no simple relationship between providing IT capabilities and realizing IT-enabled benefits. Continuous monitoring and control are necessary in the iterative process to adjust projects (including additions, modifications, and deletions) until final capability delivery and benefit realization are achieved.

Phase 4—Closing the IT-Enabled Program: This phase emphasizes two key themes: reviewing the benefits realization of the program and analyzing the lessons learned during the execution process of the IT-enabled program. The key to closing an IT-enabled program lies in reviewing the benefit realization that genuinely reflects the organization's strategic goals. If the program's benefits decrease or are no longer needed due to organizational strategy or environmental changes, the program may be terminated. Regardless of the reason for termination, steps should be taken to close the program.

Five Principles of IT-Enabled Program Management

The five principles of IT-enabled program management are critical to the success of a program. Each principle provides important guidelines for managing the program. These principles not only help the program management cope with rapidly changing business environments but also ensure that the program can effectively support the long-term strategic goals of the enterprise and ultimately achieve organizational transformation. Next, the specific content and importance of each principle in practical application are explained.

Maintain Alignment with Business Strategy—Dynamic and Adaptive

External drivers, such as market fluctuations, may cause frequent changes in business strategy direction. A program must exhibit sufficient flexibility and adaptability to keep pace with strategic changes and dynamically adjust its goals. Therefore, a program needs a robust and flexible working environment to handle frequent boundary changes. However, these changes still must be applied to the program in a controlled and managed manner. The Business Case for the program should comprehensively consider potential scenarios and, once approved, should be periodically reviewed to ensure ongoing strategic alignment.

A Clear Vision for the Program and Stakeholder Communication

The primary purpose of an IT-enabled program is to achieve transformational change or significantly advance the organization's future capability.

To reach a favorable future state, the program's leaders must articulate a clear vision for the entire program in its early phases. Clarity is a key trait that ensures the program remains aligned with the organization's strategy. For instance, if the vision changes due to environmental change or technological advances, it may indicate substantial changes in the program itself, necessitating a reassessment of original goals. Besides creating a clear vision, program management requires continuous communication of the program's vision among all stakeholders to gain and retain commitment and support. A program without a clear vision will confuse stakeholders about future goals, reducing the chances of success.

Focus on Benefits and Risk Management

The core program management task is coordinating all related activities to achieve strategic objectives and realize the final benefits. Therefore, the program's scope, including related projects and activities, is set to achieve the expected benefits. Organizations will assess the program's success based on the realization of benefits and its continued relevance to the strategic environment. When expected benefits have strategic value, effective risk management becomes crucial. However, programs often focus too much on daily operations and project activity issues while neglecting organizational strategy and long-term challenges, leading to failure and not realizing the benefits. Hence, including benefit management as a primary task of program governance ensures effective management of benefits and risks. If management determines that the program is not generating sufficient value, they should consider terminating it.

Design and Deliver Consistent Benefit Realization Capabilities

A program must clearly define the organizational capabilities to be delivered in the Program Blueprint and instill them in the business operations according to an established schedule to achieve maximum improvement while minimizing any negative impact on daily operations. If the organization's needs change during the program's life cycle, the Program Blueprint and expected organizational capabilities should be adjusted accordingly. If organizational strategy changes resulting from the expected capabilities

appear unrelated, the program's feasibility should be questioned and per-
haps terminated. Additionally, the program should provide clear project
guidance, regularly review the execution to ensure consistency with the
Program Blueprint, and strive to smoothly transition the program's outcomes to the business operations department.

Learning from Experience and the Environment

Programs are learning-oriented but temporary organizations. A program
continually reflects and improves its performance throughout its life cycle. When program team members possess a learning mindset, the overall
performance improves. Practical learning benefits from built-in review
mechanisms at key checkpoints, allowing management team members
to absorb and share both productive and failed experiences, thereby promoting the continuous advancement of the program. Therefore, an organization's ability to learn from experience is often critical to its program
management capabilities.

Core Functions of the IT-Enabled Program Managers

Responsibilities for IT-Enabled Program Managers

While many companies lack a unified approach to digital transformation,
various roles, such as Senior IT Director, Digital Transformation Director, Head of Digital Transformation, Digital Transformation Manager,
and IT-enabled Program Manager, often share a common responsibility:
coordinating and managing multiple digital projects to achieve specific
digital transformation strategic goals. The Program Manager must lead,
organize, and manage the IT-enabled program until the corresponding
digital capabilities are delivered, achieving the expected digital benefits
and concluding the IT-enabled program. It is essential to emphasize that
the IT-enabled program focuses on developing digital capabilities and,
more importantly, transforming these capabilities into organizational
benefits, ultimately achieving value enhancement. Figure 1.4 illustrates
the linkages an IT-enabled Program Manager must maintain to fulfill
their responsibilities: upward alignment, downward alignment, and interfacing connection.

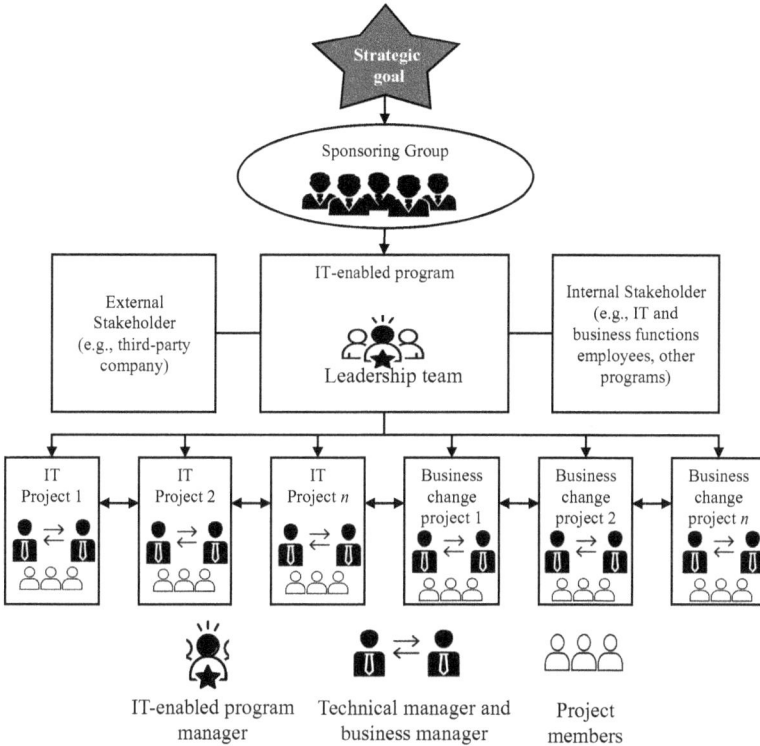

Figure 1.4 Organizational level control diagram of digital transformation program

The Upward Alignment Responsibility

When a company decides to embark on a digital transformation, it formulates corresponding strategic goals for digital transformation. The initiators of the digital transformation, as key stakeholders (often the company's top executives), establish a Sponsoring Group. This Sponsoring Group decomposes the digital strategic goals into multiple, more specific digital transformation objectives and then makes investment decisions on whether to initiate specific IT-enabled programs. This group is the authority for the program and represents the top of the hierarchy in program direction, as seen in Figure 1.4.

Once the decision to initiate an IT-enabled program is made, the Sponsoring Group appoints a manager for the IT-enabled program. If the digital transformation goal is outsourced to a third-party company, the corresponding IT-enabled Program Manager will be assigned by the third-party company to take responsibility for precisely defining, leading, organizing, and implementing the program. Therefore, the first core responsibility of the IT-enabled Program Manager is to report to and communicate with the Sponsoring Group. Specific responsibilities include securing ongoing resource support from the Sponsoring Group, continuously reporting the program's progress and risks, and delivering milestone results in accordance with the Program Blueprint.

The importance of the IT-enabled Program Manager's reporting to the Sponsoring Group lies in the need for the Sponsoring Group to coordinate multiple programs simultaneously and make required changes to strategic directions. Only through this link can programs ultimately integrate to achieve the organization's digital transformation strategic goals. Especially when a specific IT-enabled program encounters problems or faces failure, the Sponsoring Group needs to make timely adjustments to prevent the organization's digital transformation strategic goals from failing.

The Downward Alignment Responsibility

In addition to reporting to the Sponsoring Group, the IT-enabled Program Manager is responsible for further decomposing the strategic goals into multiple related digital projects. This decomposition involves establishing a leadership team, including the Project Managers for each project, to coordinate the planning, organization, implementation, control, and closure of the entire IT-enabled program. Therefore, the IT-enabled Program Manager's second linkage responsibility is coordinating multiple subordinate digital projects. Specific responsibilities include local goal setting, resource allocation, conflict resolution, and integration of project deliverables.

For example, in conflict resolution and delivery integration, IT-enabled programs often include multiple digital projects that may encounter conflicts (e.g., resource conflicts, schedule conflicts, or interpersonal conflicts). Additionally, projects may operate independently, focusing solely on their project-level goals while neglecting the overall program-level goals. The result would be that individual digital projects perform well, but the overall program fails to effectively integrate the outcomes of these digital projects. For instance, a digitalization project of the R&D process and a digitalization project of the manufacturing process may lack coordination, leading to integration issues between digital R&D and digital manufacturing (such as incompatibilities in technical standards). Hence, the IT-enabled Program Manager must resolve conflicts among digital projects and integrate their deliveries to ensure the outcomes meet the Sponsoring Group's expectations.

It is essential to recognize that digital projects differ from traditional IT projects, which are often managed by technical personnel with an IT background. Technical and business aspects are equally important in digital projects that involve digital transformation and the reshaping of business processes. In many companies' digital implementation processes, the participation and cooperation of business personnel directly determine the success of the program. Thus, many companies appoint two Project Managers for each digital project: a technical Project Manager and a business Project Manager, who collaborate to achieve the digital project's goals and tasks.

The Interfacing Connection Responsibility

In addition to the upward and downward responsibilities, the IT-enabled Program Manager must maintain continuous communication and collaboration with key external stakeholders. These stakeholders include related Program Managers, leaders of departments responsible for resource allocation within the organization, leaders of business units affected by the digital transformation program, and relevant government officials outside the organization.

For example, when an IT-enabled program needs to share specific resources with a related IT-enabled program (most commonly the sharing of technical personnel), continuous communication and collaboration are necessary to ensure the smooth completion of both parties' work. Additionally, the Program Manager may need to lobby leaders responsible for resource allocation to secure a share of the limited organizational resources. Furthermore, some IT-enabled programs might outsource specific IT projects to third-party companies. In such cases, the Program

Manager's ability to maintain open communication channels with the relevant leaders of the third-party company is also crucial to the program's success.

Five Management Competencies for IT-Enabled Program Managers

IT-enabled Program Managers must first possess the foundational capabilities of traditional Program Managers. These include the ability to actively collaborate with key members within the program, establish and maintain positive working relationships, and master basic project management methods and processes, especially proficiency in using various project and program management software tools. However, managing a unique program like digital transformation requires additional critical skills not typically demanded of traditional Program Managers.

Agile Adaptation Management

In their early proposition of goal-setting theory, Professors Edwin Locke and Gary Latham posited that clear goals lead to higher commitment and easier attainment, assuming other conditions remain constant. However, the digital transformation strategic goals often exhibit Volatility, Uncertainty, Complexity, and Ambiguity (VUCA), meaning these goals cannot be clearly defined from the outset. The intangibility and invisibility of digital elements make it difficult to judge direction based on experience, posing significant challenges. This strategic uncertainty inevitably transfers to the IT-enabled Program Manager. The path to achieving digital transformation strategic goals remains unclear, highly complex, and presents multiple implementation solutions.

How does one effectively manage such challenging goals? Relying on traditional goal management thinking, theories, and methods is not feasible. An iterative approach, making adjustments as progress is made, will be essential to achieving the goals. Therefore, the first crucial skill an IT-enabled Program Manager needs is understanding the VUCA nature of digital transformation strategic goals and translating them into corresponding IT projects. Furthermore, they must be agile in adjusting the IT-enabled program (e.g., by adding, deleting, or modifying IT projects) to ensure the program can dynamically respond to adjustments and developments in digital strategic goals. Thus, an IT-enabled Program Manager must possess strong, agile adaptation management skills.

Integrated Conflict Management

One of the major challenges in managing an IT-enabled program is the interdependencies among multiple IT projects, which occur under limited resources, leading to various conflicts. These interdependencies (including goal, task, resource, and reward interdependencies) act as a double-edged sword. On the one hand, they promote collaboration among different IT projects, but on the other hand, they readily cause conflict.

Traditional methods for conflict resolution, such as avoidance, confrontation, accommodation, and compromise, are ineffective strategies. Backed by systematic research, Professors Jiang and Klein promote integrated conflict management as a core capability for resolving such conflicts. The theoretical foundation for integrated conflict management lies in constructive controversy and strategic consensus theory. An IT-enabled Program Manager can emphasize the program-level goals of digital transformation and achieve consensus on these goals within the project leadership team (including the Program Manager and Project Managers). Especially when reward mechanisms among different IT projects are interdependent, achieving consensus on goals will enhance the IT-enabled Program Manager's integrated conflict management capability, as compelling debate can lead to effective integrated conflict solutions.

Ambidextrous Management

Scholars identify a series of paradoxical conflicts at both the program and project levels unique to IT-enabled programs. These include two main categories: strategic paradoxes of technological transformation and governance paradoxes of the program. The former needs resolution by the program's Sponsoring Group, while the latter requires intervention by the IT-enabled Program Manager. The governance paradoxes include three types:

1. During the planning phase of the IT-enabled program, the program level often emphasizes agility, while subordinate IT projects seek a stable implementation environment.
2. During the governance phase of the IT-enabled program, the program level needs to effectively control multiple IT projects to ensure the entire program aligns with the digital transformation strategic goals. In contrast, subordinate IT projects desire sufficient autonomy to address technical and business challenges.
3. During the delivery phase of the IT-enabled program, the program level aims to coordinate the delivery sequence of various IT projects and ensure the effective integration of results. In contrast, individual IT projects prefer to deliver according to their initially established schedules.

The IT-enabled Program Manager must possess ambidextrous management skills to resolve conflicts between program-level and project-level goal demands effectively.

Dynamic Stakeholder Coordination

Maintaining communication with key stakeholders of the digital transformation program and continuously gaining their support is crucial for the resilience of the IT-enabled program in the face of external shocks, and thus, is a key factor in its success. Stakeholder coordination ensures that individuals who might significantly influence or be affected by the IT-enabled program must understand, participate in, and support its implementation.

For an IT-enabled Program Manager, managing key stakeholders poses challenges from two aspects. First, the complexity of stakeholders in an IT-enabled program arises from the organizational changes and restructuring involved, which inevitably affects many interests and can obstruct the program's smooth implementation or create new beneficiary groups. The manager must distinguish supporters from resisters, assess their power and influence, and gauge their interest in the program. Based on this analysis, stakeholders can be managed accordingly: Some require intensive communication and support, others need regular progress reports, and some may require confrontational measures.

Secondly, the importance of stakeholders can change dynamically during the implementation of the IT-enabled program. Formerly crucial stakeholders might become less important, while previously insignificant ones might suddenly become decisive. Therefore, the IT-enabled Program Manager must understand these dynamic changes and coordinate stakeholders accordingly, requiring strong dynamic stakeholder coordination skills.

Digital Literacy

Digital literacy refers to a leader's understanding and appreciation of digital and emerging technologies. Compared to traditional Program Managers, IT-enabled Program Managers must have a higher level of digital literacy. One of the key differences between digital leadership and traditional leadership is the emphasis on digital literacy. A digitally literate Program Manager can gain a deep understanding of the significance and value of digital transformation, effectively translating strategic goals into actionable steps.

Furthermore, IT-enabled programs inherently leverage digital technologies to transform and reshape organizations. Leaders without basic digital literacy will struggle to mediate between technical and business teams. While IT-enabled Program Managers do not need to be seasoned digital experts, they should continually learn and understand digital technologies, appreciate their value, and maintain a keen awareness of technological advancements and trends.

Essential Cognition for Learning Program Management

Understanding the importance of program management in digital transformation, as well as the roles and responsibilities of Program Managers and the required skills, helps grasp the diversity and complexity of program management work. The success of program management operations and organizational transformation has a significant impact on an organization's competitiveness. For readers beginning to learn program management and those already engaged, the following three critical concepts must be noted:

Applicability of Program Management Knowledge and Tools

Beginners often eagerly seek to learn and practice key management concepts or tools, such as organizational change, competitive advantage, benefit realization, and new business models. While these concepts and tools have significant implications, each has specific contexts and limitations. There is no *best* program management perspective applicable to every situation. For example, program management plays a significant role in executing organizational strategy during strategy-driven digital transformation. However, more extensive programs, government-led programs, or agile programs may not fit the tools provided in this book. Misunderstanding the applicability of program management can cause adverse effects. Readers must understand the contexts and characteristics of program management knowledge and tools to maximize their effectiveness.

Dynamic Nature of Program Management Work

In addition to possessing program management knowledge and tools, Program Managers must continually collect relevant information to manage programs effectively. This chapter mentions the three primary responsibilities of Program Managers: upward communication, comprehensive planning, organizing, implementing, controlling, delivering, and continuous communication and collaboration with key stakeholders. To accomplish these tasks, Program Managers must gather internal and external information to draft appropriate program plans, which need constant updates and adjustments to align with organizational goals. For instance, with the advent of the AI era, Program Managers must actively collect market demand information to adjust program plans in response to changing strategic objectives.

Keeping Program Management Knowledge Updated

Like other fields, program management knowledge continuously accumulates and advances due to changing environments, technological progress, intensifying competition, and increasing transformation demands. For instance, fierce competition emphasizes consumer needs, making customer-oriented business models more important. The rise of mobile devices requires companies to invest in new product and service delivery channels. These changes necessitate reevaluating the relevance and applicability of existing program management knowledge and tools and developing new ones. Learners and practitioners of program management must stay updated, continuously learning and absorbing the latest knowledge and tools to tackle rapidly changing environmental challenges.

A high-level perspective of the Program Manager's role is not defined by whether individual projects are completed, but by whether the intended strategy is realized. A great Program Manager is not merely an executor of strategy, but a strategic interpreter and real-time navigator. When facing constraints such as limited resources, organizational resistance, or technical bottlenecks, the Program Manager must know when to pivot, compromise, or push through—and that judgment can only come from a deep understanding of the original strategic intent and the ability to navigate changing complexities of personnel, limited resources, and organizational culture.

At the end of this chapter, we introduce a fictional case entitled "Digital Transformation of *The Sun News*." *The Sun News* case is a vivid illustration of an IT-enabled transformation. It represents a comprehensive digital transformation journey that encompasses not only the adoption of digital technologies but also cultural change, workforce transformation, and the redesign of operational and business models. This case brings to life the concepts introduced in Chapter 1 by demonstrating how a traditional media organization responded to market disruption through a coordinated and strategic approach. From rethinking core news values to restructuring the organization, introducing new digital platforms, training staff in video production, and launching digital products, *The Sun News* exemplifies how digital transformation involves profound, organizationwide changes.

The key challenges and decisions encountered in this case will be revisited and analyzed throughout Chapters 2 to 5, following the four phases of the IT-enabled program management life cycle: identifying and formulating the program, defining and planning the program, executing and delivering the program, and, finally, closing the program. By tracing the evolution of *The Sun News* through these phases, readers will gain a grounded understanding of how IT-enabled program management serves as the bridge between digital strategy and operational execution, and how it enables a "soft landing" for digital transformation efforts. As the case examples unfold in subsequent chapters, keep in mind that there is usually more than one viable approach to digital transformation. You may wish to use the information and frameworks in the chapters to develop alternate strategies and documents to the ones provided.

Discussion Items

Every reader should be able to discuss the themes and ideas of this book in a conceptual manner. However, all discussions should be tailored to the reader's level in terms of context and applicability. Discussants with experience should add depth by considering how their past, current, or future organizations are prepared to meet the demands of managing an IT-enabled transformation program from its inception to its conclusion.

1. What is the relationship between digital transformation and IT-enabled program management?
2. How does each IT-enabled program management life cycle phase connect to the subsequent phase?
3. What are the primary responsibilities of an IT-enabled Program Manager?
4. What skills are required for an IT-enabled Program Manager to meet their responsibilities? How can an organization develop those skills or lessen the necessary breadth of skills?
5. How does an understanding of the five principles of program management help an IT-enabled Program Manager?

Complementary Reading

Babbar, A., R. Janardhanan, R. Paternoster, and H. Soller. 2023. "Why Most Digital Banking Transformations Fail—And How to Flip the Odds." *McKinsey Digital.* Accessed April 17, 2025. https://www.mckinsey.com/capabilities/mckinsey-digital/our-insights/tech-forward/why-most-digital-banking-transformations-fail-and-how-to-flip-the-odds.

Bennett, N., and J. Lemoine. 2014. "What VUCA Really Means for You." *Harvard Business Review* 92 (1/2): 27.

DottedSign. 2023. "What Is Digital Transformation? Learn About the Steps and Purpose of Digital Transformation from 4 Successful Cases." Accessed February 26, 2025. https://www.dottedsign.com/zh-tw/blog/product/what-is-digital-transformation.

Gregory, R. W., M. Keil, J. Muntermann, and M. Mähring. 2015. "Paradoxes and the Nature of Ambidexterity in IT Transformation Programs." *Information Systems Research* 26 (1): 57–80.

Jiang, J. J. 2023. "From Information Technology Projects to Digital Transformation Programs: Research Pathways." *Project Management Journal* 54 (4): 327–333.

Jiang, J. J., J. Y. T. Chang, H. G. Chen, E. T. G. Wang, and G. Klein. 2014. "Achieving IT-Enabled Program Goals with Integrative Conflict Management." *Journal of Management Information Systems* 31 (1): 79–106.

Jiang, J., G. Klein, and W. Huang. 2020. *Projects, Programs, and Portfolios in Strategic Organizational Transformation.* Business Expert Press.

Kane, G. C., A. N. Phillips, J. Copulsky, and G. Andrus. 2019. "How Digital Leadership Is(N't) Different." *MIT Sloan Management Review* 60 (3): 34–39.

Locke, E. A., and G. P. Latham. 2006. "New Directions in Goal-Setting Theory." *Current Directions in Psychological Science* 15 (5): 265–268.

Matt, C., T. Hess, and A. Benlian. 2015. "Digital Transformation Strategies." *Business & Information Systems Engineering* 57 (5): 339–343.

SAP Insights. 2023. "What Is Digital Transformation." Accessed February 26, 2025. https://www.sap.com/taiwan/insights/what-is-digital-transformation.html.

Verhoef, P. C., T. Broekhuizen, Y. Bart, et al. 2021. "Digital Transformation: A Multidisciplinary Reflection and Research Agenda." *Journal of Business Research* 122: 889–901.

Vial, G. 2019. "Understanding Digital Transformation: A Review and a Research Agenda." *The Journal of Strategic Information Systems* 28 (2): 118–144.

Wu, X., G. Klein, and J. J. Jiang. 2023. "On the Road to Digital Transformation: A Literature Review of IT-Enabled Program Management." *Project Management Journal* 54 (4): 409–427.

Wu, X., X. Ma, W. Huang, and J. Jiang. 2022. "Soft Landing of the Digital
    Strategy—Digital Program Management." *Tsinghua Business Review* 1–2: 12–19.
Wu, X., X. Ma, J. Jiang, and W. Huang. 2022. "Digital Program Managers—
    New Position in the Digital Era." *Harvard Business Review (China)* 2022:
    124–129.

Case Study: Digital Transformation
of *The Sun News*

*This case is a fictional scenario. The content of the case is written in accordance
with the requirements outlined in the chapters of this book. Relevant names,
titles, and other information are manufactured and do not represent actual
events. This chapter initially describes the case, which is then carried through
the book with additional material, including illustrations of tools and techniques, discussions, and questions.*

Case Background

The Opportunity for *The Sun News*'s Transformation

In the seemingly distant past, high-quality content drove newspaper sales,
increasing the newspaper's influence and boosting advertising revenue.
However, high-quality content no longer guarantees increased newspaper
sales, and readers no longer rely solely on hard copies or even online newspapers for news. The diversification of news carriers, the proliferation of
media outlets, and the growth of digital advertising revenue significantly
changed the industry's business model.

The Sun News Publishing, which includes *The Sun News* (the flagship
newspaper), *The Evening Sun* (a supplemental daily news edition), and
Sun Online Media (their digital platform), began a digital transformation
a couple of years ago. At that time, after returning from an overseas study
tour, General Manager Ken and senior executives drafted an organizational change strategy, which was approved by Chairman Derek and Executive Directors John and Alan. Subsequently, Ken assigned Senior Vice
President Wang to communicate with reporters, explaining that The Sun

News Publishing would undergo digital integration and diversified operations to support the company's long-term development. This decision occurred during a period of drastic changes in the traditional newspaper industry, marked by a sharp decline in market demand for newspapers and the rise of digital news.

The Competitive Environment

One of the biggest challenges for news organizations transitioning from traditional newspapers to a business model dominated by digital advertising is competing for media traffic. Since 2020, major media outlets have begun live-streaming significant domestic events, marking a new era in news media storytelling. The number of clicks and viewing traffic for each news story has become a key measure of its value, posing challenges for traditional newspapers' production capabilities.

During The Sun News Publishing's digital transformation, its long-accumulated competitive advantages became obstacles to the transformation. As it stood, journalists had to choose between *traffic* and *news value*. News organizations must balance and blend these considerations to ensure the quality of their news, demonstrating the influence and reach of digital media beyond traditional print media. In this context, news organizations created new interaction modes with readers, completely changing the older news workflows.

Key Points of The Sun News's Transformation

"Everything we do is aimed at making our city better than it was in the past," Ken pointed out the core value of The Sun News Publishing's news units. The President of *The Evening Sun*, Frank, believes digital tools are like flexible limbs, enabling journalists to navigate freely in the new media era. However, the core value of news is always the muscle that supports everything; without sufficient strength, one cannot go far, much less cross towering mountains. The Sun News Publishing's transformation aimed to continue its core values of quality news reporting and not abandon the core spirit accumulated over the past 40 years.

In an interview, Frank mentioned:

The true purpose of The Sun News Publishing's transformation is not merely to pursue visible digitalization, but to let the core news philosophy of The Sun News Publishing shine in every corner of the digital world, ensuring long-term operation and making our city better with our influence.

Digital Transformation of *The Sun News*

Planning for the Future

To explore potential trends and developments in the future of the news media industry, The Sun News Publishing established a strategic research team comprising senior management and grassroots employees from various units. Their mission was to outline the future blueprint for The Sun News Publishing. After three months of research, they found that, based on various market data from the prior five years, TV contact rates in local media industry rose somewhat, from 78.2 percent to 84.6 percent, while newspaper contact rates fell annually, from 68.2 percent to 31.3 percent. During the same period, online news media contact rates increased from 32.6 percent to 67.1 percent, growing rapidly and likely to capture some of the television market share.

These figures indicate that the digital transformation of the news media industry is an inevitable trend. In many cases, the fastest path to digital transformation may be through acquiring new departments, introducing advanced technology, and hiring new talent to replace the old organizational structure, thereby moving directly into the digital work phase. However, Ken had a different perspective. He emphasized: "The transformation of The Sun News Publishing involves not only changes at the operational level but also requires all employees to transform together to realize the meaning of transformation."

According to the strategic research team's report, The Sun News Publishing outlined two main axes for future development: first, to comprehensively promote digital integration in the news media, placing The Sun

News Publishing's news content and product services on various media platforms to expand the readership, increase news contact rates, and enhance influence; second, to actively develop diversified businesses, using The Sun News Publishing's long-accumulated resource advantages to develop various services related to the core business, thereby achieving diversified operations and providing stable support for the long-term development of The Sun News Publishing's news media.

Digital Integration

Thus, in a critical decision, The Sun News Publishing embarked on its digital transformation journey. Senior Vice President of the IT Department, Tony, and Senior Manager of the Editorial Development Department, Eric, played significant roles in this transformation. They recognized that news presentation was no longer limited to TV and computer screens but increasingly appeared on smartphones. Feng, the CEO of the New Media Management Department at The Sun News Publishing, emphasized that The Sun News Publishing is moving toward *multiscreen cloud integration,* which is their new goal.

In the past, *The Sun News* and *The Evening Sun* primarily provided news to print media; however, this scenario has since changed. Not only do they need to supply print media, but journalists must also provide real-time news and video content for The Sun News Online on a daily basis. Feng foresaw that in the future, they would not only supply content to print and online media but also provide content for TV, computers, and smartphones, ensuring that readers and viewers worldwide can access The Sun News Publishing's high-quality content through different media, with content storage and transmission based on cloud technology.

However, as The Sun News Publishing decided to move toward these three different screen media, they discovered their most significant shortfall was in video content. Given that future media and video services are inseparable, The Sun News Publishing recognized the need for profound internal transformation to enter the video content field. Top management emphasized that true transformation requires the entire team to change together. Based on this idea, The Sun News Publishing began training its employees one year after the program commenced to enhance their video production capabilities, ensuring that journalists could shoot video news, edit, and produce video content.

Video Editing Training

Senior executives recognized that the actual transformation of The Sun News Publishing required all colleagues to keep pace with these changes. Based on this belief, The Sun News Publishing also began offering education and training in video self-production, aiming to familiarize journalists with the basics of shooting video news and acquiring video post-production skills.

However, getting seasoned journalists out of their long-standing comfort zones proved to be difficult. David, general manager of Sun Online Media, mentioned: "Many veteran journalists have significant gaps in IT usage. I remember one nearly 60-year-old journalist who didn't even know how to create a new folder." David and The Sun News Online team led the entire publishing house's video training courses, teaching journalists how to shoot and edit videos in the simplest ways.

For *The Sun News*'s senior news team, facing the challenges of the digital age meant starting from scratch. Senior translator Maggie was one of the representatives chosen for the digital transformation of the news department. She worked late every night, learning to use various tools on her phone. She recalled: "Initially, it took me over three hours to edit the first video news. However, as time passed, I gradually mastered the skills, reducing the time to just one-half hour." While some journalists were genuinely committed to learning video news, many produced mediocre videos to meet key performance indicators (KPIs). The Sun News Publishing's top management realized that the transformation of text journalists was too slow, so they decided to hire professional video news talent to accelerate the overall transformation process.

Establishment of the New Media Group and a Video Department, the Launch of Sun TV, and the Operation of Digital Products

Establishment of New Media Group: In the second year of the program, The Sun News Publishing underwent significant organizational restructuring, merging the "Financial Daily Business Unit" and the "Event Business Unit" to form the "New Media Group." This subgroup conducted various activities in different fields. Benefiting from The Sun News Publishing's strong corporate image, the "Exhibition Marketing Integration Business" became a new revenue source for the group. The events department of the early Social News, which gathered many professionals, was integrated into The Sun News Publishing's "Event Business Unit" after the Social News ceased operations. Considering the rapid decline in advertising revenue, holding various events and providing sponsorship have become effective strategies to increase income.

Establishment of Video Department: Meanwhile, The Sun News Publishing also established a dedicated video business department to advance video content production and development. They invited Bella to serve as the chief operational officer and invested in building a professional video news team. This department built studios and purchased advanced hardware and software equipment. In July of that year, The Sun News Publishing conducted a large-scale recruitment effort, emphasizing the demand for video skills.

Launch of Sun Shopping Group: Early in the program, The Sun News Publishing expanded into e-commerce, investing millions to create the "Sun Shopping Network" online shopping platform. They positioned it as a one-stop shopping website, offering a wide range of products based on consumer demand, with a focus on local features and representative products. The "Sun Shopping Group" highlighted features such as high-strength information security policies, partnerships with local travel operators, and the establishment of a specialty section to attract consumer attention. This shopping network aims to provide a comprehensive shopping experience, meet diverse customer needs with over 100,000 product choices, and deeply explore local characteristics.

Launch of Sun TV Channel: To further strengthen The Sun News Publishing's video brand image, The Sun News Publishing received government approval to launch Sun TV. Sun TV was not intended to be a traditional TV station; it offers diverse real-time services, including video, text, and images, with an emphasis on integrating and developing search, interaction, and social features. The launch of Sun TV also marked the gradual improvement and development of the video department, reducing the demand for text journalists to shoot videos and further adjusting KPI strategies from pressure to rewards, encouraging the creation of high-quality content.

Operation of Digital Products: Early on, The Sun News Publishing equipped each employee with the latest tablet and subsequently launched its first digital product, the "Sun News" App. Deputy Editor-in-Chief Cathy took over the redesign and optimization of the App. The editorial department established a new media center, aiming to complete the app's update and launch within a few months. To achieve this goal, Cathy allocated resources from various centers within the editorial department. She invited Deputy Director Steven from the local center and Deputy Director Tom from the interview center to participate in the product planning. Later, two colleagues from the editorial center and ten young members joined, making the team more complete and gradually shaping the product. At that time, *The Sun News*, *The Evening Sun*, and Sun Online Media jointly invested in developing this App, fully supporting the project. Initially, the team had a traditional newspaper mindset, but after multiple discussions, they shifted their focus to user experience, ensuring the design met users' needs.

News Distribution Based on Audience Segments

Beginning late in the second year, The Sun News Publishing conducted internal staff rotations to cultivate digital media capabilities. These rotations focused on training digital production teams and helping journalists become more familiar with digital content delivery methods. In the same year, the editorial department launched its second digital application, the "Sun News+" App, primarily targeting professionals over 30, providing them with curated news content twice daily. Tim, then Deputy Editor-in-Chief of *The Sun News*, led this digital transformation and the birth of "Sun News+." He shared: "The initial intention of Sun News+ was to shift from 'mass communication' to 'targeted communication' for specific audiences." To ensure the smooth operation of "Sun News+," *The Evening Sun*'s then Editor-in-Chief, Roy, invited Steven from the interview center to lead the product's operations. Director Lin stated, "I also want to prove that as a veteran journalist, I can successfully transition to the digital field." Since then, he has fully committed to the digital realm, focusing mainly on online content and making digital adjustments to news based on the digital production team's requirements.

Digital Platform Integrated Editing Desk: Starting in the second year, The Sun News Publishing carried out a series of organizational restructurings. The editorial departments of *The Sun News* and *The Evening Sun* were merged into the "Sun News Department," and a new position, Chief Content Officer, was created, held by then Editor-in-Chief Thomas. Although they still operated as two separate teams, the new structure placed a greater emphasis on digital content. Based on this, the news department established website traffic (PV) as an important KPI at the beginning of year 3, prompting journalists to pay more attention to publishing timing and the impact of social media sharing. Senior Manager of the IT Department, Vida, revealed: "To ensure journalists can publish promptly, the news department established the 'Digital Platform Integrated Editing Desk,' which primarily ensures smooth digital platform operations and trains junior managers to meet the demands of digital news."

CHAPTER 2

Identifying and Formulating the Program

Chapter 1 introduced the four phases of the program life cycle. This chapter delves into the first phase, *Identifying and Formulating Programs*. As shown in Figure 2.1, this phase is divided into two parts: (1) Identifying the Pre-program, which is directed at pulling together program leadership and creating strategic direction for the IT-enabled program, and (2) Formulating the Program to build and document a consensus of intent among the leaders. Explicit authorization, leadership roles, and tools enable decisions that fully align the program with organizational strategy.

Identifying the Pre-Program

Initiating the Organizational Transformation Strategy

When environmental changes present opportunities or threats to the organization, necessitating transformational change, the organization's leadership must devise new strategies. Based on these newly designated strategies, the necessary tasks and objectives to achieve the organization's goals are set. At this point, the need to initiate a program becomes evident. The new organizational strategy serves as the impetus for launching the program, which enables the organization to execute its strategy effectively. The program's goal is to achieve the objectives outlined in the organizational strategy.

Appoint the Program Sponsor

Once the need for a program is recognized, a member of the organization's leadership will act as the Program Sponsor, initiating the program

Phase I Main Tasks	Governance Control
1) Identifying the Pre-program a) Initiating the Organizational Transformational Change Strategy b) Establishing the Sponsoring Group c) Establishing the Program Management Team d) Planning the Pre-program	1. Sponsoring group supervision and authorization 2. Ensuring the Program Brief aligns with organizational strategy
2) Formulating the Program a) Developing the Program Strategy Map b) Developing the Program Mandate c) Developing the Program Brief d) Developing the Program Preparation Plan	**Key Roles** 1. Sponsoring Group 2. Senior Responsible Owner **Phase I Deliverable Document** 1. Program Mandate 2. Program Brief 3. Program Preparation Plan
3) Approval to Proceed	

Figure 2.1 Main tasks of identifying and formulating programs

life cycle. The Program Sponsor is the senior manager who first realizes the need for organizational change, has expectations for the organization's future state, and is responsible for the organization's success or failure. They handle preliminary tasks before the program enters the board's discussion, compiling information on the changes the organization faces and why the program is necessary.

Draft the Program Vision

In the early phases of the program, the Program Sponsor must develop a broad vision of the program, conveying the organization's future state once the program's objectives are achieved. This statement is referred to as the Program Vision. The Program Vision outlines the future state of post-program delivery, aiming to attract more stakeholders and secure their support and commitment. After drafting the initial Program Vision based on the organization's strategic goals, the Program Sponsor discusses it with key stakeholders (e.g., the board) to seek resources and authorization for establishing the program.

Establishing the Sponsoring Group

When the Program Sponsor identifies that the organization's strategic objectives require execution through a program and has a draft vision for the program, the program is brought to the attention of key organizational stakeholders to obtain initial funding and approval to proceed. The Program Sponsor should invite several supportive stakeholders to join the Sponsoring Group at the time of initiation.

A program requires continuous organizational leadership support to secure and maintain necessary investments and resources. The Sponsoring Group, invited by the Program Sponsor, consists of members interested in the program from a strategic perspective and have decision-making power over the organization's investments and capital expenditures, influencing the program's progress (e.g., board members and heads of operational departments).

Appoint the Senior Responsible Owner (SRO)

The first task after forming the Sponsoring Group is to appoint the SRO. The Sponsoring Group should promptly appoint the SRO to lead the program, enabling them to oversee subsequent program formulation tasks. The SRO becomes responsible for the program's success. They hold the highest managerial authority within the program and should possess the necessary authority, reputation, experience, and skills to lead and guide the program.

During the program identification and formulation phase, the SRO's tasks include establishing and communicating the program vision, providing leadership and direction, and securing investments and funding. In the definition and planning phase, they ensure the feasibility of the program's Business Case. During the execution and delivery phase, the SRO certifies the realization of expected benefits, maintains contact with key stakeholders, monitors risks, and makes certain that the program aligns with the organization's strategic direction.

Establish the Program Governance Board

Once an SRO is officially appointed, their first task is to form a support team, the Program Governance Board. Large programs may impose a heavy workload on the SRO. In such cases, the Sponsoring Group should support the SRO in recruiting and organizing other individuals holding appropriate expertise. The SRO will appoint and chair the Program Governance Board to participate in early program activities and establish governance mechanisms. The board consists of individuals with managerial responsibilities and decision-making authority within the organization. Their selection influences whether the program can achieve its expected goals. For example, members are senior executives from functional departments responsible for providing essential resources for the program. This structure helps effectively address issues that may arise during the execution of change activities within the program.

Subsequent tasks of the Program Governance Board include monitoring program management to ensure that it proceeds as planned, reviewing and tracking program progress, and controlling progress to deliver the planned outcomes and benefits. The board must secure resources and specific commitments to support the SRO in advancing the program.

Establishing the Program Management Team

After the SRO establishes the Program Governance Board, the executive governance layer of the program is complete. Subsequently, the program formulation tasks begin. As the highest responsible person, the SRO is accountable for the program's success, overseeing direction, review, approval, and supervision at every phase of the life cycle. Thus, the SRO needs a Program Management Team to handle the program's management layer.

The SRO requires assistance from a Program Management Team during the initial program activities. Initially, this team requires only a few key core members, such as the Program Manager, Business Change Manager, and heavily impacted functional managers, to assist the SRO in completing the tasks of the first phase, *Identifying and Formulating the Program*.

The Program Management Team plans and executes the program's first-line activities, following the SRO's leadership to complete the identification, formulation, definition, and planning phases. They manage the program and deliver the expected benefits in accordance with the program plan. During the implementation phase, the Program Manager assigns tasks to team members based on the program plan and is responsible for ensuring the program's deliverables and benefits are realized.

Appoint the Program Manager

When forming the Program Management Team, the SRO should prioritize appointing the Program Management Team leader, the Program Manager. The Program Manager should have a change-oriented mindset, distinct from the goal-oriented thinking typical of Project Managers. They need strategic orientation and adaptability. The Program Manager must possess the necessary credentials and reputation to undertake the role's responsibilities, understand the program's goals, and lead the Program Management Team in completing the planned tasks.

The Program Manager leads and manages the program, maintaining communication with the Program Governance Board, delivering new capabilities, and realizing benefits throughout the program's duration. During the program identification and formulation process, the Program Manager assists the SRO in developing the Program Brief and Program Preparation Plan. In the program definition and planning phase, the Program Manager leads the Program Management Team in formulating the program's Business Case. Upon approval, the Program Manager executes and delivers the program, continuously reviewing and updating the Business Case to achieve program goals.

Recruit Program Management Team Members

Members of the Program Management Team should possess appropriate skills, knowledge, and experience in program management. As the program plan becomes clear, the need for staffing becomes evident, and the Program Management Team may expand accordingly. We have provided the case examples in Table 2.1.

In the case of *The Sun News*'s digital transformation, the organizational change strategy involves moving toward a digitally integrated new media center and developing diversified operations to support the sustainable development of the newspaper industry. Ken, General Manager of The Sun News Publishing Headquarters, acts as the Program Sponsor. His drafted Program Vision Statement mentions, "Enabling *The Sun News* to reach readers through digital media." To this end, Ken established a Sponsoring Group, including Derek, John, Alan, and unit heads such as Steven and Frank.

Table 2.1 *Pre-program activities example for* **The Sun News's** *digital integration program*

Activity	Case example
Initiating the Organizational Transformational Change Strategy	Moving toward a digitally integrated new media center Diversified operations supporting sustainable development
Appointing the Program Sponsor	Ken, general manager of The Sun News Publishing Headquarters
Drafting the Program Vision Statement	Ensuring *The Sun News*'s news reaches readers through digital media
Establishing the Sponsoring Group	**Chairman:** Derek **Board Members:** John, Executive Director Alan, Executive Director **Senior Executives:** Ken, General Manager of The Sun News Publishing Headquarters Steven, President of *The Sun News* Frank, President of *The Evening Sun*
SRO	Ken, General Manager of The Sun News Publishing Headquarters
Establishing the Program Governance Board	Steven, President of *The Sun News* Frank, President of *The Evening Sun* David, General Manager of Sun Online Media Feng, CEO of the New Media Management Department Tony, Senior Vice President of IT Department
Appointing the Program Manager	Wang, Senior Vice President of The Sun News Publishing Headquarters
Program Manager Recruits Program Management Team Members	Thomas, Editor-in-Chief of *The Sun News* Roy, Editor-in-Chief of *The Evening Sun* Eric, Senior Manager of the Editorial Development Department Vida, Senior Manager of IT Department

Ken was subsequently appointed as the SRO by the Sponsoring Group and formed the Program Governance Board. This board includes David, Steven, Frank, Feng, and Tony. Senior Vice President Wang was appointed as the Program Manager responsible for *The Sun News*'s digital transformation plan. Wang then established the Program Management Team, comprising Thomas, Roy, Eric, and Vida, which led the team members in completing the program's planning and execution tasks.

Planning the Pre-Program

Once the Program Manager has recruited the members of the Program Management Team responsible for executing the planning tasks, the pre-program planning can commence.

Develop the Organizational Strategy Map

An Organizational Strategy Map aims to *visualize* and *concretize* the organizational strategy, facilitating smoother communication among the Program Manager, the Sponsoring Group, and other stakeholders. Based on the organization's strategic goals, the Program Manager must conceive the program (i.e., change activities) to execute the organizational strategy, with the program's goals derived from the organizational strategy. The Program Manager then preliminarily identifies the change activities required to achieve the program goals and presents the relationships between these activities, program goals, and organizational strategy objectives in a visual format.

In the case of *The Sun News*'s digital transformation, as shown in Figure 2.2, the organizational goal of *The Sun News* is to achieve sustainable development. Two main transformation strategies were designed to reach this goal: digital integration and diversified operations. Subsequently, the necessary change activities to achieve these goals were preliminarily designed based on these transformation goals.

Identify and Analyze Stakeholders

After the Program Manager presents the Organizational Strategy Map, they should identify and analyze the stakeholders who may influence the achievement of organizational goals based on the Strategy Map. Throughout the program life cycle, stakeholders may change. The Program Manager needs to identify who might have an impact during the program life cycle, and additional stakeholders (both internal and external) that will be impacted by the program should be identified. Based on the Organizational Strategy Map's change activities, stakeholders interested in the organizational strategy can be identified. Evaluating the potential impact on the program's development of stakeholders allows for the creation of

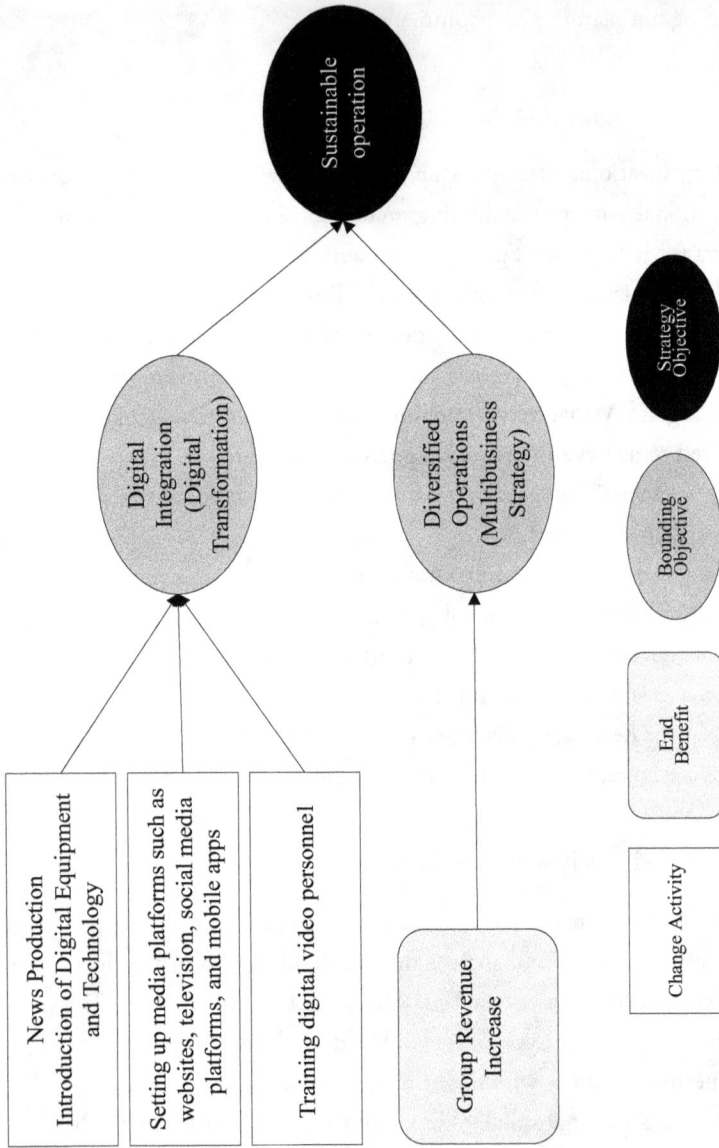

Figure 2.2 The Sun News's Organizational Strategy Map example

Table 2.2 Program Stakeholder Map

Organizational Strategy Map change activities Key stakeholders	Change activity A	Change activity B	Change activity C	Change activity D
Stakeholder A		X	X	
Stakeholder B	X	X	X	X
Stakeholder C				X

a Stakeholder Map. As shown in Table 2.2, the Stakeholder Map can be used to identify and document key stakeholders in each change activity. Based on the identified key stakeholders, the Program Manager will assess whether to include them in the program organization or processes to ensure the smooth advancement of the program. Table 2.3 provides an example of a Stakeholder Map for *The Sun News*.

Analyzing stakeholders involves understanding their impact on the program's outcomes, their associated interests, and the importance and power of each stakeholder. The purposes of stakeholder analysis are:

- To understand the influential power that stakeholders hold in the program.
- To assess how the program impacts the interests of stakeholders.

Based on these two purposes, stakeholders can be analyzed using the Power–Interest Grid (Figure 2.3). This analysis helps to determine how to interact with specific stakeholders. In addition, since a program may have many stakeholders, organizing them by role is beneficial for management (e.g., governors, influencers, resource providers, and beneficiaries). Stakeholders can either support or hinder the program's benefits, depending on their level of involvement and participation.

High Power, High Interest (Manage Closely): These stakeholders are directly affected by the program's planning, as program planning activities might impact their plans, and the program's output will likely impact their daily operations. For example, the digital integration goals of *The Sun News* directly affect the interests of *The Sun News*, *The Evening Sun*, Sun Online, and the Information Department. The managers of

Table 2.3 Stakeholder Map example for The Sun News *digital transformation*

Organizational Strategy Map change activities Key Stakeholders	Digital integration of news production	Setting up media platforms (websites, TV, social media, mobile apps)	Training digital video personnel
Internal stakeholders			
Decision Makers and Senior Managers (Level 1)			
Derek, Chairman	X	X	
Steven, President of *The Sun News*	X	X	X
Frank, President of *The Evening Sun*	X	X	X
David, General Manager of Sun Online Media		X	
Tony, Senior VP of IT	X	X	
Senior VP of HR			X
Department Level 2 Managers, Senior Managers			
Feng, CEO of the New Media Management Department	X	X	
Thomas, Editor-in-Chief of *The Sun News*	X		X
Roy, Editor-in-Chief of *The Evening Sun*	X		X
Eric, Senior Manager of the Editorial Development Department	X		X
Vida, Senior Manager of IT	X	X	
Senior Manager of HR			X
Employees			
Local News Editors			X
Reporters			X
External Stakeholders			
Readers or Users		X	
Advertisers	X		
IT Solution Providers	X		

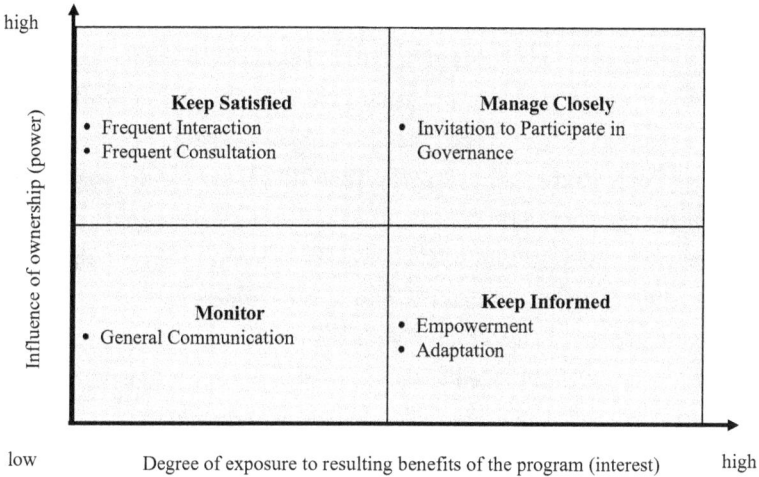

Figure 2.3 Stakeholder power and interest matrix

these affected departments have significant power within the organization and can influence the progress and delivery of the digital transformation program. Without their endorsement and support, advancing the program may be challenging. It is advisable to invite these stakeholders to participate in the program's governance, provide them with frequent updates, and involve them in key decision-making processes.

High Power, Low Interest (Keep Satisfied): These stakeholders have a high level of influence over the program, but the program's outcomes have little impact on their interests. For example, the digital integration goals of *The Sun News* do not directly affect the Marketing Department or departments involved in multifaceted business transformation goals. However, these department heads will still be impacted by the planning of the digital integration program in their daily tasks, and their power within the organization may also affect the program's progress. It is essential to interact with them regularly, keep them informed about the program's progress, and involve them as consultants when necessary.

Low Power, High Interest (Keep Informed): The outcomes and benefits of the program significantly affect their interests, but they have limited influence over the program. They are a group affected by the program, impacting their daily work and ability to adapt to future organizational changes. They should be kept informed and treated with respect. Regularly update this group of stakeholders on the program's information, provide training on using new technologies, and otherwise assist them in adjusting to the organization's future state.

Low Power, Low Interest (Monitor): These stakeholders have limited influence over the program, and its outcomes have minimal impact on their plans or operations. They should still be notified of the basic information about the program to ensure they understand the program's objectives and any changes that might affect them. Communication must remain open, as continual changes to the organization and environment may alter their status in subsequent phases.

We provide examples based on the stakeholders identified in *The Sun News*'s digital transformation case and their roles in the program (as analyzed using the stakeholder power and interest matrix in Table 2.4, with results shown in Figure 2.4).

After identifying and analyzing stakeholders, the Program Manager should compile the information from the stakeholder analysis into a Stakeholder Profile document. This document should record the names and roles of each stakeholder, as well as their respective group names. Through the Stakeholder Profiles, the Program Manager can understand stakeholder habits, interests in change activities, their impact on outcomes, and the outcomes that interest them in the program.

Refine the Program Vision Statement

During the early portion of the *Identifying and Formulating the Program* phase, the Program Sponsor drafted a Vision Statement for the program. To further develop this Vision Statement, interactions with the identified key stakeholders should begin after they have been identified. The Vision Statement should be shared to explain the post-reform or transformation state to the stakeholders, helping them understand the overall context. Subsequently, the Vision Statement should be discussed in detail to achieve a consensus on the future state. This process will clarify the program's significance to all parties involved and help avoid vague objectives. Table 2.5 provides an example of a Vision Statement from *The Sun News* digital integration program.

Table 2.4 *Stakeholder Profile example for* The Sun News

Internal stakeholders	Interest in change activities	Impact on final outcome	Specific benefits of digital transformation	Personal information
Decision Makers and Senior Managers (First-Level Supervisor)				
Derek, Chairman	Introduction to digital equipment and technology for news production, including setting up media platforms such as websites, TV, social media platforms, and mobile apps.	• Organizational strategy development and resource allocation	• Enhancing the competitiveness of enterprises • Getting higher returns • Corporate sustainability	• Caring for staff • Ready to hand over the baton to Ken. • Support Digital Transformation
Steven, President of *The Sun News*	Introduction to digital equipment and technology for news production; setting up media platforms such as websites, TV, social media platforms, and mobile apps; training for digital audiovisual personnel.	• The Key to Successful Transformation • The division's product-related revenue accounts for approximately 40% of the organization's current revenue, and its employees make up 50% of its headcount.	• Increase in divisional revenue • Departmental digital capability enhancement • Diversity of news topics	• Twelve years with the company • Interested in joining the Board of Directors • Loves a challenge • Emphasize teamwork • He went to college with Ken.
Frank, President of *The Sun News* and *The Evening Sun*	Introduction to digital equipment and technology for news production; setting up media platforms such as websites, TV, social media, and mobile apps; training for digital audiovisual personnel.	• The Key to Successful Transformation • The division's product-related revenue accounts for approximately 30% of the organization's current revenue, and its employees comprise 30% of the organization's headcount.	• Increase in divisional revenue • Departmental digital capability enhancement • Diversity of news topics	• Parachuted in to take over the post for just over two years. • Comfortable with the status quo • Frequent complaints about insufficient resources • Frequently sparring with Steven

(continued)

Table 2.4 Stakeholder Profile example for The Sun News *(continued)*

David, Sunline General Manager	Setting up media platforms, including websites, TV, social media, and mobile apps.	• Expanding and deepening the application of digital technology is the key to the success of the transformation. • The division's product-related revenue accounts for approximately 20% of the organization's current revenue, and its employees comprise 10% of the organization's headcount.	• Expansion of departmental scale • Raising the importance of the department in the organization	• Ten years with the company • Information technology background, former general manager of an information technology company • Doctoral Degree in Progress • Imaginative and curious about new technologies
Senior Vice President, Human Resources Department	Digital Audiovisual Personnel Training	• Overseeing the human resources structure of the entire organization, providing human resources planning for organizational change, and ensuring logistical support.	• Digital Human Resources Reinvention • Enhancing the effectiveness of the organization's human resources	• Fifteen years with the company • Frequent staff training and cohesion enhancement activities • Taking care of junior staff • Worried about the human resources implications of the digital transformation.
Tony, Senior Vice President, Information Technology Division	Introduction to digital equipment and technology for news production, including setting up media platforms such as websites, TV, social media platforms, and mobile apps.	• Oversee the IT structure of the entire organization, providing IT planning for organizational change and ensuring logistical support.	• IT Resources Reinvention • Planning the organization's long-term IT transformation	• Twelve years with the company • Going through the informatization phase of the company • Positive thoughts on digital transformation

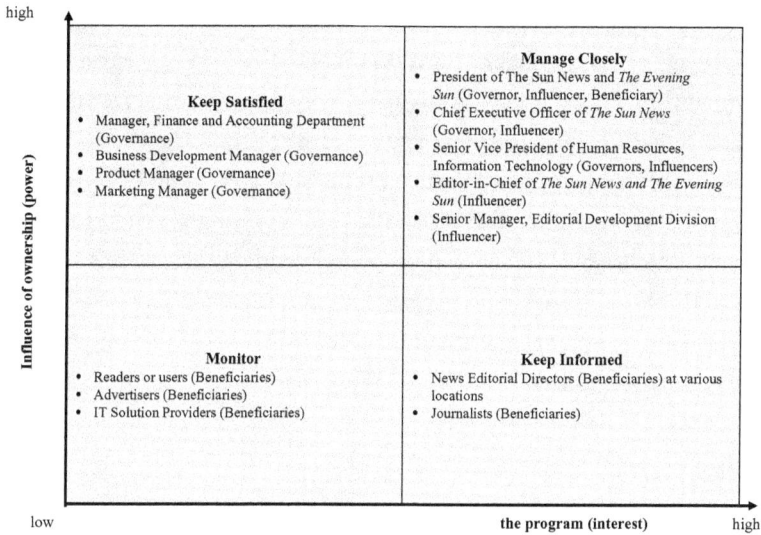

Figure 2.4 *Power and interest matrix example of* The Sun News

Table 2.5 The Sun News's *digital integration program vision example*

Vision statement	Case example
Drafted Program Vision Statement (by the sponsor)	To integrate *The Sun News*'s news into readers' lives through digital media.
Revised Program Vision Statement	To focus on the digital integration of the news department, providing digital news to readers to access *The Sun News*'s news across various platforms. Additionally, to diversify operations, ensuring that *The Sun News*'s core journalistic values continue to shine in every corner of the digital world.

In the case of *The Sun News*'s digital transformation, as shown in Figure 2.2, the organization's strategic goal is to achieve sustainable operations. The original two transformational goals in the Organizational Strategy Map, *Digital Integration* and *Diversified Operations*, were revised following stakeholder identification and analysis, as well as the revision of the Program Vision Statement. Ultimately, digital integration was chosen as the primary goal of the program.

For *The Sun News*'s senior managers and decision makers, connecting with readers through the newspaper is the primary way to maintain revenue. However, environmental changes and technological developments affecting reading habits have led to a significant decline in newspaper readership. Through digital transformation, they hope to enhance the company's competitiveness and achieve higher returns. Department heads and senior managers are concerned with improving their department's performance and efficiency. Employees must improve their skills and value while maintaining job stability amidst changes. Readers and users want higher-quality digital news content and more convenient access to it. Therefore, focusing on digital integration for *The Sun News*'s news department is essential and the most direct way to stabilize and increase the number of readers. It will also improve department performance and efficiency, enhance corporate competitiveness, and achieve high returns.

Formulating the Program

Program management is part of the project management discipline, and both approaches emphasize creating temporary organizations that are internal to the host organization to deliver specific outputs or changes that benefit the overall organization. The management of projects and programs differs in terms of increased agility, responsiveness, controls, and resources to properly conclude the program, which faces more significant levels of strategic importance, complexity, uncertainty, and scope. Still, many of the concepts from project management apply to programs, including the need to formulate and articulate an initial purpose, plans, and structure. To seek approval to initiate a project, a charter is created that contains sufficient detail to support a decision on commencement. Similarly, a well-formulated program requires setting strategic objectives, making necessary commitments, and promising specific outcomes. The documents created in this section serve as the Program Charter seeking approval from authorized stakeholders.

Developing the Program Strategy Map

After the Program Manager completes the stakeholder analysis, understands the stakeholders' influence, interests, and impact on the program, and revises the Program Vision Statement based on communication with stakeholders, they develop the Program Strategy Map. The Program Strategy Map will align with the stakeholders' expectations for the organization's future, given that the stakeholders' expectations regarding the program are known at this stage.

Purpose of Program Strategy Map

The Program Strategy Map is a visual tool to:

- Cement the relationship of the organization's strategic goals to the program, demonstrating the program's necessity within the organizational strategy.
- Ensure that each project within the program aligns with the program goals, converting the organization's strategic goals into executable projects.
- Show how each project contributes to the overall program goals.
- Assist in better decision making.
- Help key stakeholders perceive the attractiveness of the future state and the competitive advantage that the organization can gain from the program.

Content of Program Strategy Map

The Program Strategy Map should include:

- The organization's strategic goals
- Program goals: The program's goals should be derived from the organization's strategic goals, and the program's purpose should be specifically described.
- Program outcomes: The outcomes required to achieve the program goals should be presented in this map. Achieving a program goal may involve integrating multiple outcomes.
- Projects required to achieve the expected outcomes: Identify the key projects necessary for the program based on the assessed outcomes.

As shown in Figure 2.5, after communicating with stakeholders, the Program Manager confirms that the program's goal is digital integration. Based on the revised Program Vision Statement, the initial outcomes identified for the program include increased unique visits by digital media readers, higher web page click-through rates, increased engagement on social media platforms, and higher mobile app click-through rates. To achieve these outcomes, *The Sun News* plans to implement digital production equipment and technologies for news production, establishing multiple media platforms, including web pages, television, social media platforms, and mobile apps.

Developing the Program Mandate

Based on the Program Strategy Map, the Program Manager identifies the prerequisite elements to achieve the program goals. Using these elements and other available information (such as projects), the Program Manager and the program management team members create the Program Mandate to lay the foundation for the program's initiation. Approval of the Program Mandate gives the program management team the responsibility and authority to acquire the necessary resources. The following details the purpose and content of the Program Mandate, with Table 2.6 providing an example based on *The Sun News* digital integration program.

Purpose of Program Mandate

The purpose of the Program Mandate is to:

- Describe the results required from the program based on the organization's strategic goals, outlining the program's vision, scope, expected budget, and timeline.
- Ensure that the program management team understands their responsibilities and executes tasks in accordance with the program's goals and requirements.

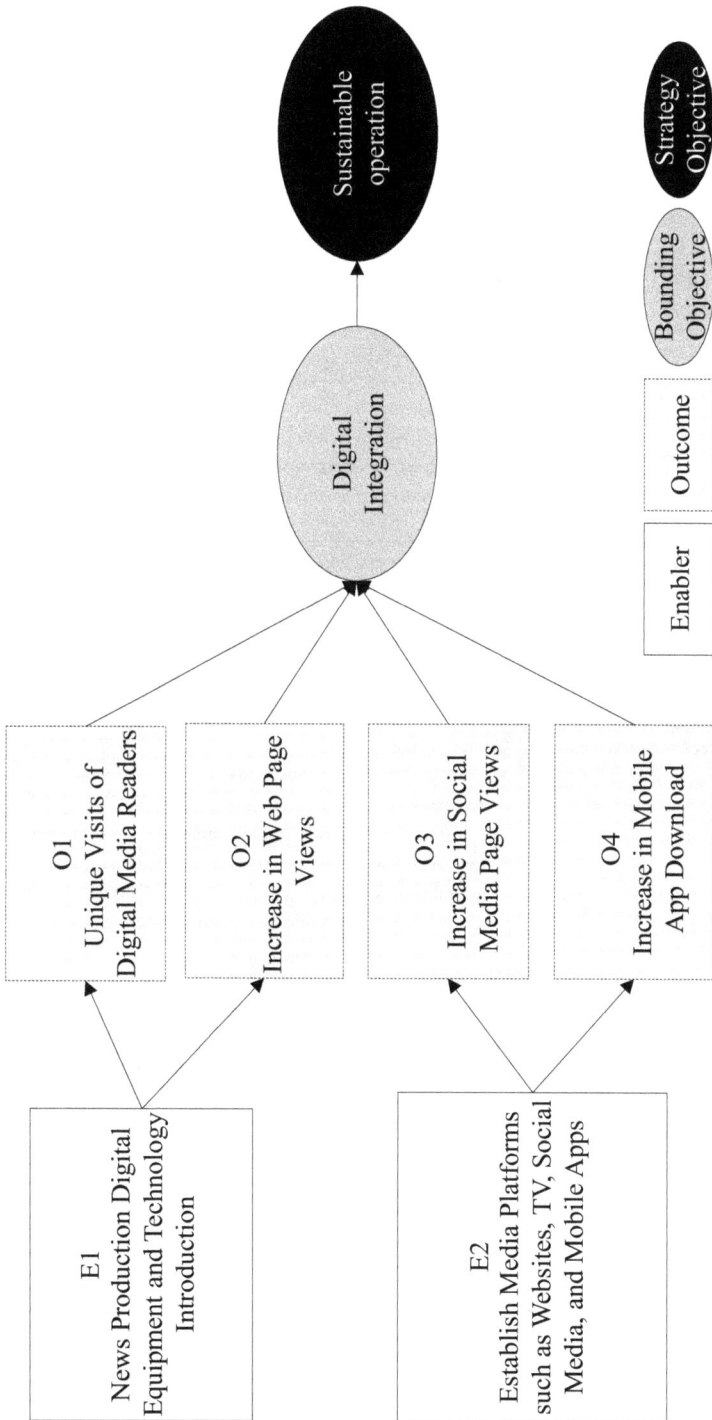

Figure 2.5 The Program Strategy Map example of The Sun News's digital integration program

Table 2.6 The Program Mandate of The Sun News's *digital integration program*

Program Mandate content	Case example
Program background	**Environmental background:** News delivery methods are no longer reliant solely on newspapers. Readers' reading behaviors have undergone significant changes, shifting from print media to mobile phones, computers, televisions, and other media, thereby altering the business model of newspapers.
The organization's strategic goals	**Digital integration:** • Implement media digital transformation and accelerate the deployment of future media. • Ensure *The Sun News*'s high-quality content and services are accessible across various media platforms. • Increase the reach and impact of *The Sun News*'s news content.
Program vision	Focus on the news department's digital integration to provide readers with digital news, enabling them to access *The Sun News*'s content across various platforms. Additionally, moves toward diversification ensure that *The Sun News*'s core journalistic values continue to illuminate every corner of the digital world.
Current organizational state and desired future state	**Current state:** • *The Sun News* has not yet responded to external environmental changes with corresponding transformations. The company relies primarily on newspapers as its primary revenue source and lacks digital transformation-related video production talent, equipment, and resources to produce digital content. **Future state:** • Future media will be inseparable from video services. *The Sun News* must transition to an environment with video capabilities, requiring a thorough internal transformation and change. *The Sun News*'s journalists should be capable of filming video news, possess post-production skills, and be able to provide real-time news updates.
Program Strategy Map	[see Figure 2.5]

Program Mandate content	Case example
Program deliverables	**Increase in the themes and quantity of video news:** • By training print journalists in video news production, *The Sun News* (1) equips print journalists with basic concepts of shooting video news, (2) enhances video post-production skills, (3) develops digital awareness and skills among print journalists, and (4) familiarizes them with digital tools to improve the quality and quantity of video news. **Optimizing video news production processes:** • By adding management positions such as CEO, Chief Convergence Officer, and Chief Strategy Officer, you can efficiently integrate the editorial team and accelerate the pace of digital adoption. **Maintaining various digital media channels and platforms:** • Transform current print news into digital channels, enabling *The Sun News*'s high-quality news to reach a wider audience through various means, including video. Users will have multiple media options to read and interact with *The Sun News* at any time and from anywhere.
Approaches to achieve the program goals	**Training journalists in video news production:** • Provide print journalists with basic concepts of shooting video news, enhance post-production skills, and cultivate digital awareness and skills. **Adding management positions:** • By adding positions to integrate the editorial team more efficiently and accelerate digital adoption. **Establishing digital platforms:** • Provide users with multiple media options to read and interact with *The Sun News* at any time, from anywhere. **News digitization:** • Transform current print news into digital channels, enabling *The Sun News*'s high-quality news to reach its audience through various means, including video, continually.
How new services/ capabilities improve the organization	• Improving news production processes and increasing production efficiency • More diverse topics and news presentation methods • More interaction with readers • Building a talent pool ready for future trends • Attracting more audience members (quantity) • Increasing audience engagement

(continued)

Table 2.6 The Program Mandate of The Sun News's digital integration program (continued)

Program Mandate content	Case example
Program boundaries	• Diversified operations • Exploring new ventures
Expected timetable, cost budget, and potential constraints	**Timeline:** • 2019: Introduction of digital equipment and technology for news production and video training for print journalists. • 2020–2021: Development of video media platforms and operation of digital products. **Costs:** • Video training expenses: US$**650,000** • Digital video production equipment: US$**3.3** million • Establishment of digital platforms and products: US$**1.7** million • Personnel allocation and recruitment: US$1 million **Potential constraints and deadlines:** • Resistance and rejection from internal personnel • Operational budget limitations • Technical limitations in video production and platform development • Need for continuous learning of new software technologies and skills to keep up with rapid technological developments • Conflicts between digitalization goals and journalistic values

Content of Program Mandate

The Program Mandate content serves as the foundation for initiating and defining a program. It outlines the strategic justification for the program and provides a high-level view of its intended direction and outcomes. This section presents the key components that collectively define the rationale, scope, and strategic alignment of the program. These elements ensure a comprehensive understanding of why the program exists, what it aims to achieve, and how it aligns with the organization's strategic objectives.

- Program background: Explains the reasons for initiating the program, focusing on the impact of external environmental factors and pressures. The organization's strategic goals reflect the need for organizational change in response to external environmental stimuli, leading to the formulation of new strategic directions and the strategic goals necessary to achieve the desired new state.

- Program vision: Communicates the program's ultimate goal and provides an external impression of the ideal future state. At the initial phase of the program, one or more threats or opportunities related to organizational strategy will be identified. The organization's response to these opportunities or threats will form the program's vision. These driving factors will be described in the Program Mandate and later formally developed into the Vision Statement in the Program Brief.

- Current state and desired future state: Describes the organization's current and anticipated new state after achieving the organization's strategic goals through the program.

- Program Strategy Map: Based on the organization's strategic goals, the program vision, and the anticipated future state, the preliminary Program Strategy Map should describe the relationship between the organization's strategic goals and the program.

- Program deliverables: Explains the new services or capabilities through which the program will help the organization achieve its strategic goals.

- Approaches to achieve program goals: Details the tasks necessary to help the program achieve its goals, which may develop into project activities in the future.

- How new services/capabilities improve the organization: Describes the benefits that the new services or capabilities produced during the program execution will bring to the organization, which can develop into the desired benefits or benefit measurements in the future.

- Program boundaries: Specifies what project activities are excluded from this program, i.e., work that is not required to achieve the program goals.

- Expected timetable, cost budget, and potential constraints: Estimates the time, cost, and potential constraints that could impact the program's execution based on the information provided.

Developing the Program Brief

The Program Mandate, prepared by the Program Manager and reviewed by the Program Governance Board, outlines the program's vision, scope, expected budget, and timeline, ensuring the program management team understands their responsibilities. The Program Brief is based on the approved Program Mandate and is prepared by the Program Manager, followed by review and approval by the Program Governance Board. The following details the purpose and content of the Program Brief, with Table 2.7 providing an example based on *The Sun News* digital integration program.

Table 2.7 The Program Brief of The Sun News *digital integration program*

Program Brief content	Case example
Program Vision Statement and Objectives	**Vision Statement** • Provide readers with digital news available on different platforms, ensuring that *The Sun News*'s core values can shine in the digital world. **Objectives:** • Enhance video capabilities (TV, computer, mobile devices) to enable *The Sun News* to reach more users through digital media, meeting their reading habits and needs, and continuing the journalistic spirit of *The Sun News*.
Overview of program benefits	• Increase in print advertising revenue • Increase in newspaper and magazine sales revenue • Increase in digital advertising revenue • Increase in reader numbers (audience size) • Increase in total news page views • Diversification of video news topics • Improvement in video news quality • Increase in news accessibility (channels and platforms)
Benefit measurements	• Growth rate of revenue • Reader numbers (audience size): Monthly increase in users • Page views: News browsing volume (PV) • Diversification of video news topics: Setting video KPIs • Improvement in video news quality: Establishing a threshold for assessing whether video content meets publishable standards • Increase in news accessibility (channels and platforms): User satisfaction

Program Brief content	Case example
Expected timeframe for achieving benefits	The benefits begin to form gradually as the program is executed. The timeframes listed here indicate the expected time points for the benefits to reach their targets, not the start of benefit formation that year. **Year 1:** • Diversification of video news topics • Improvement in video news quality • Increase in news accessibility (channels and platforms) **Years 1 and 2:** • Increase in reader numbers (audience size)—50% annual growth • Increase in total news page views—50% annual growth **Year 3:** • Increase in print advertising revenue—30% annual growth • Increase in newspaper and magazine sales revenue—30% annual growth • Increase in digital advertising revenue—30% annual growth
Project list	• Introduction of digital equipment and technology for news production • Establishment of media platforms such as websites, TV, social media, and mobile apps
Performance evaluation post-transformation	• Journalists' skill requirements shift from writing and graphic design to video production and user experience design. • News production shifts from print format to a multichannel, digital video format. • Readers transition from accessing The Sun News through a single print channel to multiple devices. • Interaction with readers shifts from one-way to two-way, enhancing search and social functions. • Organizational team structure shifts from independent departmental operations to rotational and multidepartmental collaboration systems.
Estimated costs, time, and workload	**Personnel Training and Deployment (One-Year Completion):** • Plan video training to develop print journalists' video news production capabilities • Add management positions • Build the digital transformation video capabilities and environment for *The Sun News* **Development of Video Media Platforms and Digital Products (One-Year Completion):** • Establish a video business unit to plan digital product development • Introduce digital video production equipment and product development technology • Launch an online video platform

(continued)

Table 2.7 *The* **Program Brief** *of* **The Sun News** *digital integration program (continued)*

Program Brief content	Case example
Risks, issues, and constraints	**Risks and Issues:** 1. Personnel resistance to change leads to attrition 2. Conflicts and resistance regarding video KPIs 3. Redesign of news production processes 4. Growth in personnel video capabilities keeping pace with digital product processes 5. Loss of core journalistic values 6. Capturing lost readers and directing them to digital products **Constraints:** 1. Operational budget limitations 2. Technical limitations in video production and platform development 3. Conflicts between digitalization goals and journalistic values

Purpose of Program Brief

The main difference between the Program Brief and the Program Mandate is that the Program Brief provides information for evaluating feasibility. Its primary purposes are:

- Expanding upon the contents of the Program Mandate and reasserting the current organizational situation.
- Defining the program's goals, expected benefits, potential risks, cost estimates, and timelines.
- Avoiding laborious and time-consuming detailed cost analysis, investment evaluations, expenditure forecasts, and similar tasks in low feasibility cases.

The information provided in the Program Brief should be sufficient to determine whether the proposed change should be managed as a program, clarify the benefits the program can achieve, and provide a basis for evaluating the program's feasibility. For instance, proceeding with further planning may be pointless if the anticipated benefits are unlikely to be realized within a reasonable timeframe. During the creation of the Program Brief, all participants must comprehensively understand the current situation, identify potential conflicts (e.g., one proposed project may reduce the outcomes of another), and recognize any missing or unrecognized projects. Once approved, the Program Brief becomes a crucial foundation for developing the complete Business Case and management information for the program.

Content of Program Brief

The Program Brief expands upon the initial mandate by providing a more detailed and structured outline of the program. It refines the program's direction, clarifies its intended benefits, and establishes a framework for execution and evaluation. This section introduces the key elements that define the scope, strategy, and expectations of the program. These components ensure a comprehensive and realistic plan for delivering strategic value and guiding the program toward successful implementation.

- Program Vision Statement and Objectives: The Program Vision Statement clearly articulates the program's ultimate goals.
- Overview of program benefits: Benefits refer to the improvements or enhancements that the program's outcomes bring to the organization. This section should outline the types of benefits or improvements expected.
- Benefit measurement: Describes how the benefits will be measured, possibly presented as a Benefit Map.
- Expected timeframe for achieving benefits: Estimates the timeframe during which the benefits are likely to be realized.
- Project list: An initial list of candidate projects or required activities, a rough timeline, and any explanations for potential project termination (main projects).
- Post-change performance evaluation: Assesses the current organizational state and the performance of current business operations affected by the changes.
- Estimated costs, time, and effort: Estimates the costs, time, and effort required to design, manage, and execute the program from initiation to delivery and realization of benefits.

- Risks, issues, and constraints: Identifies any known risks associated with the program, existing issues that might impact program execution, and any known constraints, assumptions, or conflicts that could affect the program.

Developing the Program Preparation Plan

The primary purpose of the Program Brief described earlier is to provide information for the feasibility analysis of the program. Once the Program Brief is approved and the program's feasibility is assessed, the Program Manager will begin preparing the Program Preparation Plan. This Program Preparation Plan will then be reviewed and approved by the Program Governance Board. The following details the purpose and content of the Program Preparation Plan, with Table 2.8 providing an example based on *The Sun News* digital integration program.

Purpose of Program Preparation Plan

The Program Preparation Plan differs from the Program Brief in that it details the resources and management approach required for the program, aiding in the management of the complexity of the next phase—*Defining and Planning the Program*. The top purposes of the Program Preparation Plan are:

- To plan the program's governance arrangements, resources, and expected timeline.
- To identify the specific skills and experience required from participants.
- To determine the resources needed to develop the Program Blueprint and deliver the defining and planning phase of the program.
- To explain how assurance will be applied during the *Defining and Planning the Program* phase.

Content of Program Preparation Plan

A detailed preparation plan helps clarify and reduce uncertainty and ambiguity in the program's initial phase, allowing the Program Governance Board to fully understand and commit to providing the estimated costs,

Table 2.8 The Program Preparation Plan of The Sun News *digital integration program*

Program Preparation Plan content	Case example
Description of program outputs	**Introduction of Digital Equipment and Technology for News Production** • Includes the introduction of digital video production equipment, the establishment of a video business unit, and the creation of a professional video news team. **Establishment of Media Platforms such as Websites, TV, Social Media, and Mobile Apps** • Attract users who read news online, learn and understand the habits of modern audiences, and build *The Sun News's* digital brand. This will increase users' familiarity with *The Sun News's* online services and digital transformation, as well as the transition from traditional print news production to incorporating TV thinking and the logic of Internet users.
Resource requirements	**Personnel** • Need for endorsement of project leaders and change managers, and approval of personnel for new departments. **Technology:** • Video production technology, digital media development technology **Budget:** • Funding for the upgrade of digital video production hardware, training funds for journalists in video production, recruitment funds for new digital video talent, funds for establishing new businesses, and funds for digital product technology development
Governance and control	• Weekly project briefings hosted by the Program Manager with all Project Managers • Monthly meetings chaired by the Program Sponsor with business unit heads and Project Managers to confirm the program direction based on actual needs
Activity schedule	**Year 1**: Through the activities below, *The Sun News's* video capabilities and environment will be built for digital transformation and video news production. • Train print journalists in video news production • Introduction of digital equipment and technology for news production **Years 2 and 3**: Plan and operate newly launched digital news products through the below activities, building *The Sun News's* digital brand. • Establish media platforms such as websites, TV, social media, and mobile apps

(continued)

Table 2.8 The Program Preparation Plan of The Sun News digital integration program (continued)

Program Preparation Plan content	Case example
Members of the program governance board	• Steven, President of *The Sun News* • Frank, President of *The Evening Sun* • David, General Manager of Sun Online • Feng, CEO of *The Sun News*'s New Media Management Department • Senior Vice President of HR • Tony, Senior Vice President of IT
Estimated workload and costs	1. Adjusting News Production Processes **Workload:** • Improvement of news production processes • Staff education • Coordination of resistance and discomfort among staff **Costs:** • Meeting time for establishing new news processes • Adaptation costs for news process changes • Fees for hiring training instructors • Communication costs with stakeholders 2. Adjusting Organizational Structure (Adding positions such as CEO, Chief Convergence Officer, and Chief Strategy Officer; Establishing Video Business Unit) **Workload:** • Adding related management positions • Coordination of resistance and discomfort among staff • Establishing new teams, recruiting new talent, and training newcomers • Strengthening team-building activities **Costs:** • Coordination costs between units • Opportunity costs of personnel redeployment • Transition costs for personnel replacement • Costs of new management positions 3. Personnel Rotation Mechanism (Cultivating Multimedia News Content Literacy) **Workload:** • Establishing rotation mechanisms • Selecting suitable talent • Cross-departmental coordination • Education and training for each department **Costs:** • Coordination costs between units • Opportunity costs of personnel redeployment • Costs of talent cultivation • Adaptation period and resistance to new roles

Program Preparation Plan content	Case example
	4. Establishing Video KPIs for Performance Assessment **Workload:** • Training print journalists in video production capabilities and introducing basic video equipment • Setting new KPIs • Redefining journalist roles • Coordination of resistance and discomfort among staff • Adding related management positions **Costs:** • Funding for upgrading digital video production hardware • Funding for training journalists in video production • Coordination costs between units • Opportunity costs of personnel redeployment
Assurance arrangements	**Defining the Scope of Assurance:** • The scope should encompass introducing video equipment and technology, establishing the video business unit, creating the video news team, and setting up media platforms, including websites, TV, social media, and mobile apps. Ensure that project activities align with and meet the project objectives. **Developing an Assurance Activity Plan:** • Monitor program performance, identify and manage risks, assess compliance with regulations and standards, and evaluate the effectiveness of controls and processes to ensure optimal outcomes. Consider factors such as project schedule, costs, resource requirements, and personnel. **Assigning Assurance Responsibilities:** • Based on the project's scale, complexity, and impact, assign either internal or external assurance teams to conduct assurance work. For example, the Program Governance Board can assign specialists to monitor and review program performance and identify and manage risks. **Establishing an Assurance Communication Plan:** • Set up regular assurance reports and communication mechanisms to track the progress of program activities, ensuring all stakeholders clearly understand the project's progress and outcomes. **Establishing an Assurance Activity Evaluation Mechanism:** • Regularly evaluate the effectiveness of assurance activities during the project's execution and adjust as needed. For example, through regular program performance reviews, assess whether project activities meet project objectives and identify any potential issues and risks.

time, and resources listed in the Program Preparation Plan. The main content includes:

- Description of program outputs: Describe the deliverables for the program according to the defined requirements.
- Resource requirements: Specify the necessary resources and their sources (e.g., personnel, budget).
- Governance and control: Describe the governance and control methods to be applied to the team.
- Activity Schedule: Provide a timeline for achieving program and activity outputs.
- Members of the Program Governance Board: List the composition of the Program Governance Board.
- Estimated workload and costs: Estimate the workload/activities required for the program execution and the projected costs for each activity.
- Assurance arrangements: Define the assurance arrangements for *Defining and Planning the Program*. Assurance verifies and confirms that the program activities and results meet the program's objectives, requirements, and standards. Assurance activities typically include monitoring and reviewing program performance, identifying and managing risks, assessing compliance with regulations and standards, and evaluating the effectiveness of controls and processes. Assurance can be provided by internal or external parties independent of program management and delivery teams to enhance objectivity and fairness. The ultimate goal is to ensure that the program progresses smoothly in delivering the expected benefits and outcomes and to instill confidence in all stakeholders regarding the program's progress and eventual success.

Approval to Proceed with Phase 1 Outputs

In the first phase, *Identifying and Formulating the Program*, the deliverables include the Program Strategy Map, Program Mandate, Program Brief, and Program Preparation Plan. During this review and approval step, the review will assess the scope and objectives of the program, as well as its ability to deliver and achieve the expected benefits. Upon successful review, when the program receives formal approval, the Program Sponsor confirms that the program meets business needs, and the Program Governance Board commits to supporting the governance tasks throughout the program delivery process. The Program Brief and Program Preparation Plan set the task environment and direction for the program in the second phase of the program life cycle, *Defining and Planning the Program*, which will be discussed in the next chapter. Until then, the following checklist identifies the tasks to be completed in phase 1, which have been defined and illustrated in this chapter.

Risk Considerations

Risk management during the initial phase of a program life cycle—Identifying and Formulating the Program—is critical, as many strategic uncertainties and structural ambiguities exist at this stage. The primary concern here is clarifying ambiguity, surfacing unknowns, and laying a solid foundation for future planning.

At this point, the program team is often operating with incomplete information while making strategic assumptions about objectives, benefits, resource needs, and stakeholder alignment. As such, the Program Brief must include an initial set of identified risks and unresolved issues, along with possible mitigation or response strategies. These risks might relate to stakeholder resistance, unclear scope boundaries, insufficient sponsorship commitment, or unrealistic expectations regarding resources, timelines, or organizational readiness.

In the case of emergent programs, additional risks are inherited from preexisting or uncoordinated initiatives that now fall under the program's governance. These inherited risks—such as misaligned objectives between previously independent projects, unresolved technical debts, or unmanaged stakeholder tensions—must be carefully examined and documented during this phase.

Failure to assess risks early on can lead to potential creeping disruptions in later phases, such as flawed program design, delayed approvals, or even the failure of the entire program. Therefore, conducting a preliminary risk workshop, engaging key stakeholders in open dialogue about risks, and actively documenting those findings are recommended practices. Major risks and unresolved issues—both anticipated and inherited—should be stated in the Program Brief, serving as the foundation for a responsive and resilient program strategy going forward.

Checklist

Confirmation items	Check
• Develop a new organizational strategy to identify the goals of the program.	
• The Program Sponsor establishes a sponsorship group to gain support for initiating the program.	
• Appoint a Program Sponsor to start the identification and task assignment of the program.	
• The Program Sponsor establishes a Program Governance Board to gain support and assistance from department heads.	
• The Program Sponsor appoints a Program Manager.	
• The Program Manager establishes a Program Management Team.	
• The Program Manager creates an Organizational Strategy Map linking organizational strategy to program objectives.	
• The Program Manager identifies and analyzes stakeholders.	
• The Program Manager prepares Stakeholder Profiles.	
• Relevant stakeholders have participated in the program communication.	
• The Program Manager revises the Program Vision Statement.	
• The Program Manager creates a Program Strategy Map.	
• The Program Manager prepares the Program Mandate.	
• The Program Manager prepares a Program Brief to confirm the program's feasibility.	
• The Program Manager prepares a Program Preparation Plan.	

Discussion Items

When considering the discussion questions, go beyond providing a conceptual or definitional response and relate them to your experiences. Determine and critique the presence and accomplishment of these activities in your organization. If you have project-level experiences, address any similarities or differences to familiar practices.

1. What are the primary tasks of the Program Sponsor in the early phase of identifying a program?
2. What are the primary tasks of the Program Manager in the program establishment phase?
3. What is the purpose of the Program Strategy Map?
4. What is the purpose of the Program Mandate?
5. What is the purpose of the Program Brief?
6. What is the purpose of the Program Preparation Plan?

Complementary Reading

Fernandez, W., G. Klein, J. Jiang, and R. M. Khan. 2022. "Integration Networks in IT-Enabled Transformation Programs." *International Journal of Managing Projects in Business* 15 (6): 913–937.

Jiang, J. J. 2023. "From Information Technology Projects to Digital Transformation Programs: Research Pathways." *Project Management Journal* 54 (4): 327–333.

Jiang, J. J., J. Y. T. Chang, H. G. Chen, E. T. G. Wang, and G. Klein. 2014. "Achieving IT-Enabled Program Goals with Integrative Conflict Management." *Journal of Management Information Systems* 31 (1): 79–106.

Jiang, J., G. Klein, and W. Huang. 2020. *Projects, Programs, and Portfolios in Strategic Organizational Transformation.* Business Expert Press.

Piney, C. 2017. *Earned Benefit Management: Aligning, Realizing, and Sustaining Strategy.* Auerbach Publications.

PMI (Project Management Institute). 2017. *The Standard for Program Management.* 4th ed. PMI.

The Stationery Office. 2011. *Managing Successful Programmes (MSP).* 4th ed. AXELOS.

Wu, X., G. Klein, and J. J. Jiang. 2023. "On the Road to Digital Transformation: A Literature Review of IT-Enabled Program Management." *Project Management Journal* 54 (4): 409–427.

CHAPTER 3

Defining and Planning the Program

This chapter transitions to the second phase of the program management life cycle: *Defining and Planning the Program*. The Program Business Case produced in this second phase is based on the outputs from the prior phase, specifically the Program Mandate, Program Brief, and Program Preparation Plan. The Program Business Case details the resources and scheduling information required to deliver new capabilities and achieve benefits, serving as the final decision point for program continuation before the expenditure of resources in the subsequent phase: *Executing and Delivering the Program.*

The main tasks for defining and planning the program are illustrated in Figure 3.1. After completing the steps of *Defining and Planning the Program*, the Program Business Case must receive formal approval from the Program Sponsor and the Program Governance Board before moving to the third phase:

Developing the Program Business Case

The first phase, *Identifying and Formulating the Program,* resulted in the production of the Program Mandate, Brief, and Preparation Plan. These documents form the basis for creating the Program Business Case, which will be expanded into the overall program plan in this second phase: *Defining and Planning the Program.*

The primary purposes of the Program Business Case are:

- To confirm the scope, direction, and objectives of the program.
- To establish specific execution methods and actions required for the program.
- To define the program's costs, benefits, schedule, and risks.
- To assess the feasibility of the program and secure support.

Phase II Prerequisites
1. Program Mandate
2. Program Brief
3. Program Preparation Plan

Phase II Main Tasks

1) Develop Program Business Case
   a) Develop Program Blueprint
   b) Identify, Define, and Plan Program Benefits
   c) Developing the Project Dossier
   d) Establishing Program Governance Arrangements
   e) Developing the Program's Organizational Structure

2) Review and Approve Program Business Case

Governance Controls
1. Approval by Program Governance Board
2. Checkpoint Reviews

Key Roles
1. Program Sponsor
2. Program Governance Board
3. Program Manager

Phase II Deliverable Document
1. Program Business Case

Figure 3.1 Defining and planning the program

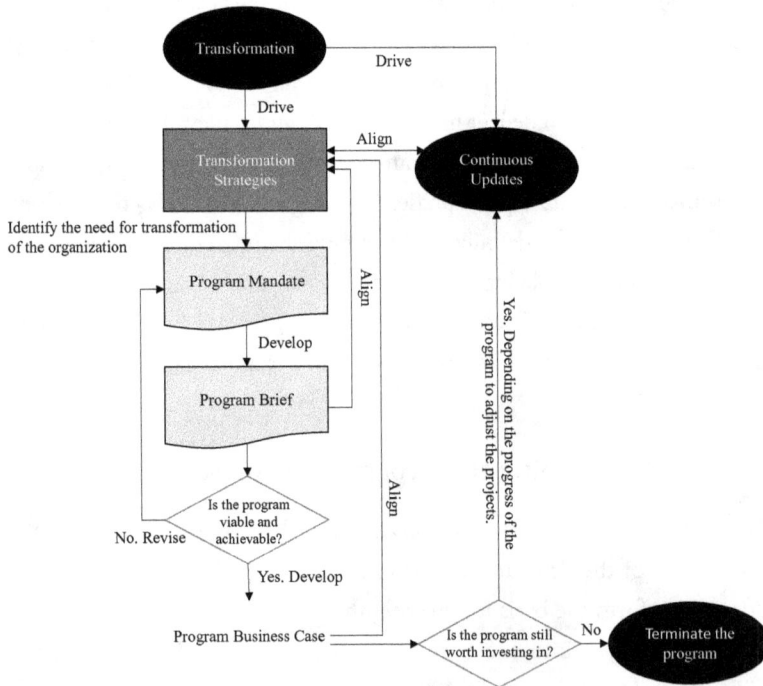

Figure 3.2 Program Business Case relationship chart

As shown in Figure 3.2, the Program Business Case evolves from the Program Mandate and Program Brief. It must align with the organization's change and transformation strategy. Throughout the program's execution, the Program Business Case must be continuously updated and dynamically adjusted based on the actual progress of the projects, changes in the external environment, and the program's overall progress. Therefore, frequent reviews and updates are required throughout the program's later execution and delivery processes.

The Program Business Case is a comprehensive collection of all information related to the program. Once the Program Sponsor and governance board approve the Program Business Case, the Program Manager must begin executing program activities based on the approved Program Business Case. The contents of the Program Business Case include:

- **Program Blueprint**: Describes the current state, anticipated future state, and gap between the current and future states.
- **Program Management Maps**: These include the Benefit Map and Benefit Dependency Map, which explain the expected benefits to be delivered and the relationships between the benefits and program activities.
- **Project Dossier**: Provides details on the projects and activities to be executed within the program.
- **Program Organizational Structure**: Describes the composition of the program organization.
- **Program Governance Arrangements**: Details the governance methods for the program.

According to the content required for the Program Business Case, Figure 3.3 outlines the planning process for the Program Business Case, describing how to plan a feasible Program Business Case. Develop a Program Blueprint from the Program Brief, set the current and future state based on the Program Blueprint, and identify the benefits needed to achieve the future state. Create a Benefit Map to illustrate these benefits. Define the measurement criteria and performance indicators for each benefit based on the relationships between the benefits outlined in the Benefit Map, and prepare a Benefit Profile. Further, a Benefits Dependency Map helps plan how to achieve the benefits by outlining the program outputs, capabilities, and outcomes from the Program Blueprint. Consolidate the projects required for the program into a Project Dossier, providing a brief overview of each project's information. Finally, present the Program Business Case to the Program Sponsor and the Program Governance Board

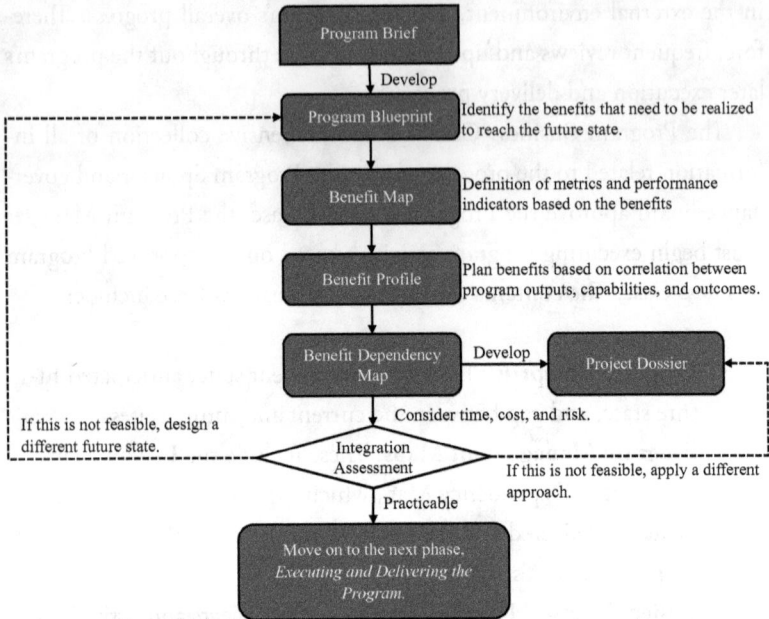

Figure 3.3 Program Business Case Planning Process

(considering time, cost, and risks) to assess the feasibility of the Program Business Case. If it is not feasible, adjust the Program Blueprint or Project Dossier as needed to iteratively design a viable Program Business Case before moving to the next phase.

Developing the Program Blueprint

Purpose of the Program Blueprint

The Program Manager develops the Program Blueprint to explain which new capabilities will emerge when the project outputs are ready to be deployed into operations and what specific outcomes the program can achieve once these new capabilities are transitioned to operational units. The Program Blueprint is illustrated for *The Sun News* case in Table 3.1 and Figure 3.4 and serves to:

- Illustrate the gap between the current state and the future state: Identify the current and future states to understand the required changes to achieve the desired outcomes (Table 3.1).

Table 3.1 Current state and future state of The Sun News *case example*

Aspect	Current state	Future state
Human resources	Existing personnel focus on single-skill print journalism, such as writing, photography, and newspaper layout.	Every journalist must be multiskilled, including writing, photography, editing, and live broadcasting abilities for digital multimedia news production.
Organizational structure	Each newspaper operates independently.	Establish new executive roles, including CEO, Chief Content Officer, Chief Convergence Officer, and Chief Strategy Officer, to integrate the news production resources and processes of *The Sun News*, *The Evening Sun*, and The Sun News Network. Create specialized units, such as the Audiovisual Department and the New Media Center, to facilitate a professional division of labor.
News production process	Editors-in-Chief of *The Sun News*, *Economic Daily*, *The Evening Sun*, and The Sun News Network operate independently.	Introduce new digital media production equipment, reorganize the editorial departments, and co-locate the editors of *The Sun News*, *The Evening Sun*, and The Sun News Network to enhance digital collaboration.
Digital news production technology	No digital news production technology in place	Integrate the resources of the editorial departments of *The Sun News*, *The Evening Sun*, and The Sun News Network to develop news production channels for three different screen mediums (TV, computer, mobile). Enhance audiovisual capabilities, products, and digital content.

- Describe requirements to support future operations: Describe the capabilities needed in the future state to support operational practices, processes, and technologies, ensuring the future operational state is well supported (Figure 3.4).
- Provide a foundation for the subsequent documents: Elaborate details for creating the Benefit Map and Project Dossier, as described later, which will guide further planning and implementation.
- Enable ongoing tracking of new capability delivery: Identifying future states provides targets for continuously tracking the delivery status of new capabilities, thereby controlling progress toward the expected operational requirements and objectives.

Future Status

Human Resources
Each reporter must have the ability to multitask. Recruit digital content product development (app design and development) professionals.

Organizational Structure
Create the Executive Director, Content Director, Convergence Director, and Strategy Director to integrate the news production resources and processes of the three newspapers and website. Established the Audiovisual Business Department and the New Media Center for division of professional labor.

News Production Process
Reorganize the editorial desk after the introduction of new digital media production equipment to improve digital collaboration. Introduce the concept of end-streaming to integrate editorial units into a content delivery platform.

Digital News Production Technology
To develop news production channels on three screens (TV, computer, and mobile phone) by integrating the resources of the three existing newspapers, one website and editorial desks of various organizations.

Projects

Video and Audio News Production Training for Text Reporters

Adjustment of corporate organizational structure

News Production Digital Equipment and Technology Introduction

Setting up media platforms for web, TV, social media, and mobile apps

New Capabilities Acquired by Project Outputs

Ability to produce audiovisual news

Improve the quality of audiovisual news content

Cross-platform/carrier delivery of digital content products

Competencies Added to the Organization

Increase in the number of topics and volume of audiovisual news

Comprehensive audiovisual news operation process

Maintaining a wide range of digital media channels and carriers

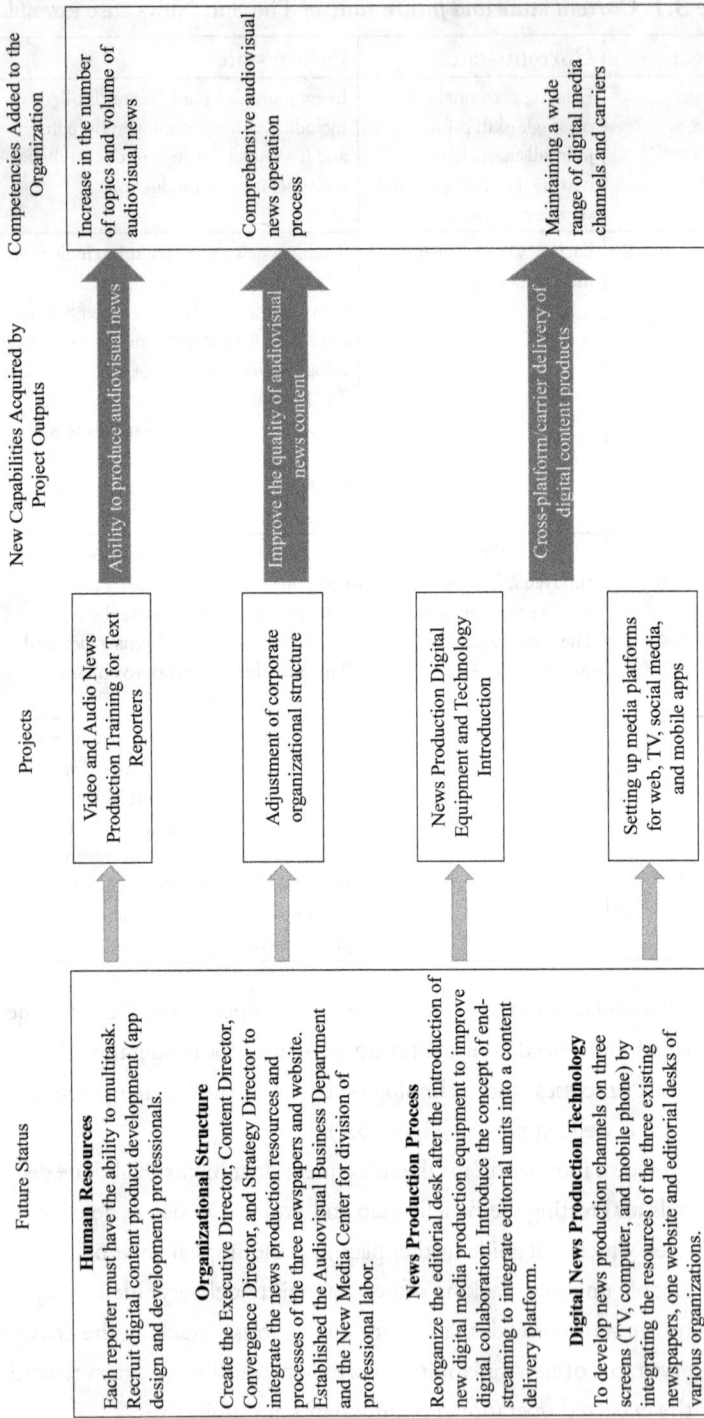

Figure 3.4 The Sun News's digital integration Program Blueprint example

Content of the Program Blueprint

As shown in Figure 3.4, the future state of *The Sun News* digital integration program is described from four perspectives: human resources, organizational structure, news production processes, and digital news production technology. To move toward this future state, four projects must be executed: training text journalists in multimedia news production, adjusting the corporate organizational structure, introducing digital equipment and technology for news production, and establishing media platforms for web, television, social media, and mobile apps. These projects aim to establish the organization's capability to produce multimedia news, improve the quality of multimedia news content, and provide digital content across various platforms and devices. Once these new capabilities are applied within the organization, they will lead to improved themes and quantity of multimedia news, a refined multimedia news operation process, and the maintenance of various digital media channels and devices.

Identifying, Defining, and Planning Program Benefits

Upon completion of the Program Blueprint, subsequent steps include:

- To identify the benefits that will be realized in reaching the program objectives.
- To define the indicators and performance metrics for measuring the benefits within the program.
- To plan the projects' outputs, capabilities, and outcomes.
- To define and prioritize the interrelationships between project outputs, capabilities, outcomes, and benefits.
- To define the performance indicators and quantitative measurement methods required to monitor benefit delivery.

The realization of benefits follows a structured framework. As illustrated in Figure 3.5, realizing benefits involves establishing new organizational capabilities through project outputs that yield desired operational outcomes when implemented, thereby realizing the expected benefits.

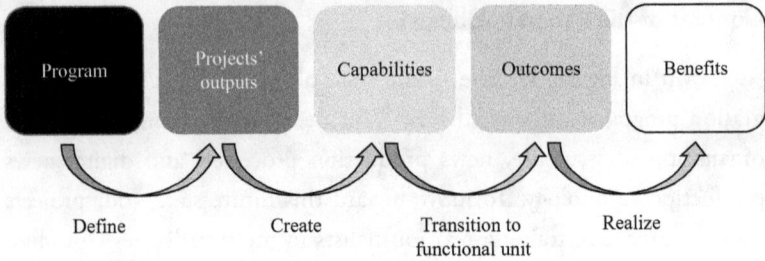

Figure 3.5 Program benefits realization framework

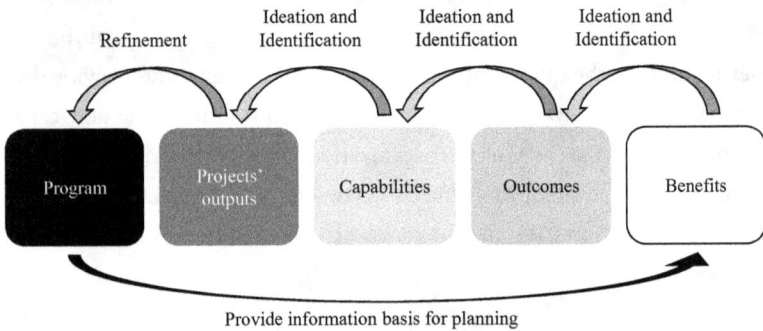

Figure 3.6 Program benefits planning framework

After defining the gap between the current and future states in the Program Blueprint, the Program Manager must define and plan the benefits that the program aims to achieve. As shown in Figure 3.6, in the method for planning program benefits, it is essential to consider the benefits required to achieve the program's objectives and then work backward to determine which operational outcomes are necessary to realize these benefits. Since the existing operational units do not fully possess the necessary capabilities to achieve these outcomes, the organization must identify which new capabilities need to be developed to achieve the desired operational results. These new capabilities depend on project outputs. After delivering the planned projects' outputs, the organization must assess whether it can achieve its goals. The backward planning approach helps Program Managers and stakeholders understand what actions must be taken to achieve the objectives. This approach ensures that the tasks required to reach the goals are planned with a clear understanding of the future targets.

Manage Program Benefits: Benefit Map

Program Management Maps help Program Managers identify, define, and plan the benefits a program should deliver. The elements of Program Management Maps include project outputs, business changes, new capabilities, outcomes, benefits, and program objectives, outlining the paths for delivering and achieving these elements, as shown in Figure 3.7. Program Management Maps encompass the Benefit Map (for identifying benefits), the Benefit Profile (for defining benefits), and the Benefits Dependency Map (for planning benefits). In Figure 3.7, we can see *The Sun News* Case example in the black blocks. Based on the initial IT project's outcome (e.g., introducing digital equipment and technology for news production), the case can lead to a business process change (e.g., adjusting the news production process). Later, based on the new equipment and new process, the case will build its new capability (e.g., audiovisual news production capability), which can provide the expected outcome, such as increasing the digital media audiences. Finally, as cumulative outcomes, the expected benefits will be realized over time, further achieving the overall program goal—i.e., enhancing digital integration revenue. The following sections will provide detailed descriptions of each.

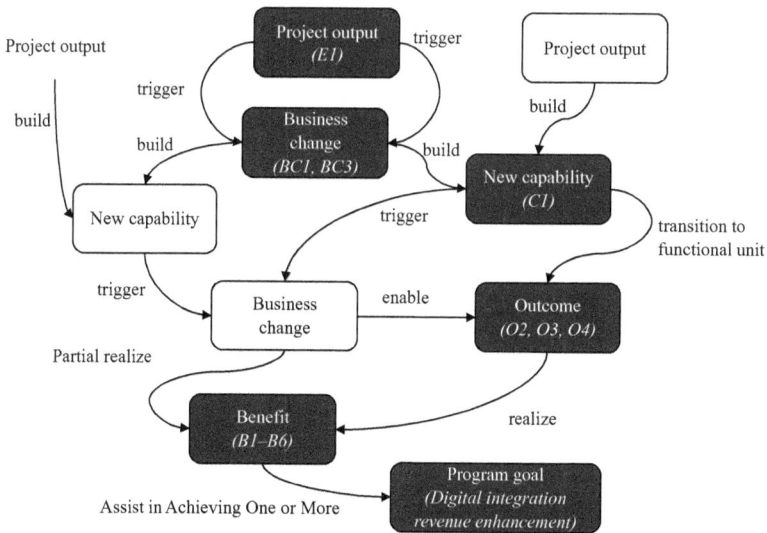

Note: *The Sun News* case example is shown in the black blocks.

Figure 3.7 Pathway to benefits and program objectives

Most benefits are realized through two fundamental types: *Enablers* and *Business Changes*. Enablers can be developed, built, or acquired, typically from outside the organization. Enablers can include personnel, processes, information, and technology, such as information systems, buildings, policies, processes, and skills. Business Changes are defined as changes in the business or operational environment, typically involving a new way of working or a new business state. Business changes should be managed as part of the benefit realization process within the program.

Some benefits or paths may not include any enablers or business changes, indicating either that enablers or business changes have not yet been identified or that no intermediate actions are required for benefit realization.

Capabilities are collections of project outputs used to deliver results. Capabilities are established within organizational operational units through project outputs, enabling the unit to accomplish tasks that were previously unattainable. The completion of specific tasks or projects often measures the success of establishing new capabilities.

Outcomes refer to the results of the change, which typically impact organizational behavior or conditions. When a change initiative is proposed, desired outcomes are anticipated. These outcomes are realized through the implementation of project activities and are visualized in the Program Blueprint as part of, or all of, the new state.

Identify Program Benefits: Benefit Map

The Benefit Map aims to *identify benefits* by progressively expanding the Program Blueprint. The Benefit Map helps to:

- Visualize benefits.
- Rationalize benefits.
- Determine the priority of benefit realization.
- Identify dependencies between benefits.
- Communicate and gain consensus with stakeholders.
- Manage and monitor the program.

Each benefit should relate to the organization's strategic goals pursued by the program. If a benefit is unrelated to strategic goals, it may distract from achieving the primary benefits. Therefore, to avoid misallocating time to less important benefits, the Benefit Map is developed to realize benefits, measure benefit costs, and assess and balance the value of benefits. A Benefit Map for *The Sun News*, as shown in Figure 3.8, will serve as the basis for our discussion of its components.

When creating a Benefit Map, the Program Manager should lead the Program Management Team and invite stakeholders to participate in discussions to create one that meets the needs of stakeholders (Fernandez et al. 2022). Creating the Benefit Map aims to identify all benefits and clarify their dependencies and importance. The Benefits Map illustrates the relationships between benefits and organizational goals, as well as the interdependencies among the benefits themselves. Benefits typically do not occur in isolation, and causal relationships exist between them. The Benefit Map illustrates the overall context of the change, showing the inputs for each benefit and how they integrate into the overall change plan.

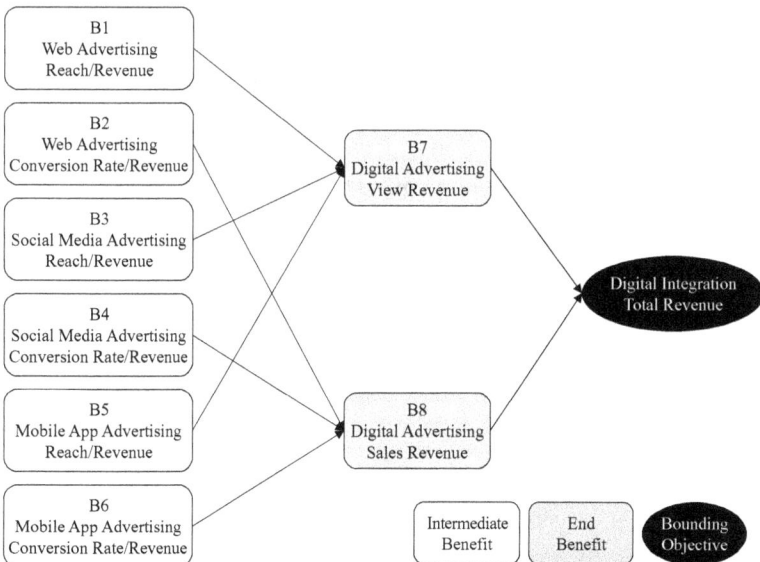

Figure 3.8 Benefit Map example for The Sun News *digital integration program*

Organizational goals are displayed on the far right of the Benefit Map. From right to left, the map encompasses the process and final benefits necessary to achieve these organizational goals, with each benefit assigned a unique number for subsequent discussion and communication. The Benefit Map facilitates planning for benefit realization by illustrating the sequence of benefit realization throughout the benefit chain. It also helps estimate the time required and plan the schedule for benefit realization. Once approved, the map is reviewed from left to right to ensure that the business changes or enablers delivering the benefits are executed correctly.

Define Program Benefits: Benefit Profile

The purpose of the Benefit Profile is to *define benefits*, and it includes the following:

- Provide measurable indicators for each benefit. The benefit indicators may be derived from the current state information provided in the Program Blueprint. Future information will include performance indicators that demonstrate the benefits achieved.
- Serve as a planning and control tool: It helps track the progress of subsequent deliveries and the realization of benefits.

Each benefit identified in the Benefit Map must be fully defined and presented in the Benefit Profile. The Business Change Manager is typically responsible for creating the Benefit Profile, identifying, developing, verifying, and managing the benefits delivery described in the program. The best way to define benefits is to involve key stakeholders who can provide various perspectives on which benefits should be achieved. Once the benefits are defined, the Program Manager can analyze the overall benefit mix, create a Benefit Profile, and possibly adjust its scope to ensure it delivers the desired balance of benefits. Table 3.2 provides an example of the Benefit Profile for *The Sun News* digital integration program. Information from the Benefits Profile is added to the Benefit Map for completion, as shown in Figure 3.9.

Table 3.2 Benefits Profile example of The Sun News *digital integration program*

Benefit ID	Benefit name	Benefit description	Benefit source	Measurement indicator	Baseline value (US$)	Target value (US$)
B1	Web Advertising Reach/Revenue	Reach rate and revenue from web advertising	Effectiveness of web ad placements	Percentage of reach and revenue growth	0.72 million/year	6 million/year
B2	Web Advertising Conversion Rate/Revenue	Sales revenue from web advertising	Effectiveness of web ad sales	Sales revenue growth	1.08 million/year	9 million/year
B3	Social Media Advertising Reach/Revenue	Reach rate and revenue from social media advertising	Effectiveness of social media ad placements	Percentage of reach and revenue growth	0.72 million/year	6 million/year
B4	Social Media Advertising Conversion Rate/Revenue	Sales revenue from social media advertising	Effectiveness of social media ad sales	Sales revenue growth	1.08 million/year	9 million/year
B5	Mobile App Advertising Reach/Revenue	Reach rate and revenue from mobile app advertising	Effectiveness of mobile app ad placements	Percentage of reach and revenue growth	0.96 million/year	8 million/year
B6	Mobile App Advertising Conversion Rate/Revenue	Sales revenue from mobile app advertising	Effectiveness of mobile app ad sales	Sales revenue growth	1.44 million/year	12 million/year
B7	Digital Advertising View Revenue	Click-through rates and revenue from combined digital advertising channels	Effectiveness of ad placements across digital channels	Percentage of views and revenue growth	2 million/year	20 million/year
B8	Digital Advertising Sales Revenue	Sales revenue from combined digital advertising channels	Effectiveness of digital ad sales	Sales revenue growth	4 million/year	30 million/year

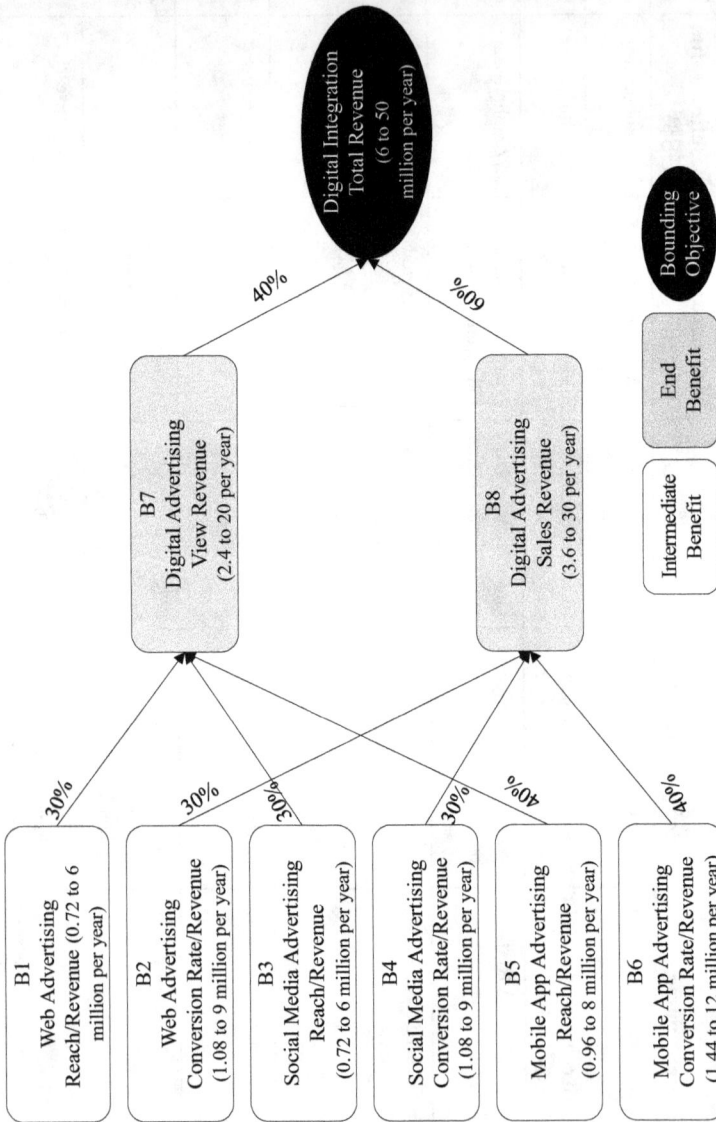

Figure 3.9 Completed Benefit Map for The Sun News digital integration program

Plan Program Benefits: Benefit Dependency Map

The purpose of the Benefits Dependency Map is to *plan benefits* by linking benefits with the related activities or changes required to achieve those benefits. This linkage helps identify and understand the changes or strategic actions needed to achieve a specific benefit (Bradley 2016). The Benefit Dependency Map introduces two additional objectives:

- Optimizing resource allocation: Visualizing how benefits are achieved helps efficiently allocate resources where they are most needed.
- Risk management refers to identifying and managing risks that might impact the expected benefits if a key activity or change cannot be implemented as planned. The Benefit Dependency Map allows for earlier identification and management of these risks.

Capabilities are established within the organization's operational units through project outputs, enabling those units to accomplish tasks that were previously unattainable. The success of establishing new capabilities is typically measured by completing the designated tasks or projects within the specified timeframe. For example, previously, *The Sun News* could not provide video news. After obtaining outputs from projects like Digital Equipment and Technology for news production and setting up media platforms, including websites, TV, social media platforms, and mobile apps, and establishing Video News Production Capability, it was able to produce video news and offer a new service to readers (see Figure 3.10 for details). Outcomes refer to the results of capability transformation. For example, after establishing the Video News Production Capability, applying this new capability to organizational behavior or conditions includes increased themes and quantity of video news, improved video news operational processes, and maintenance of multiple digital media channels and platforms (see Figure 3.10 for details).

An example of the Benefits Dependency Map for *The Sun News* digital integration program is illustrated in Figure 3.10. After identifying the final benefits B1 to B8 and process benefits, it is essential to consider

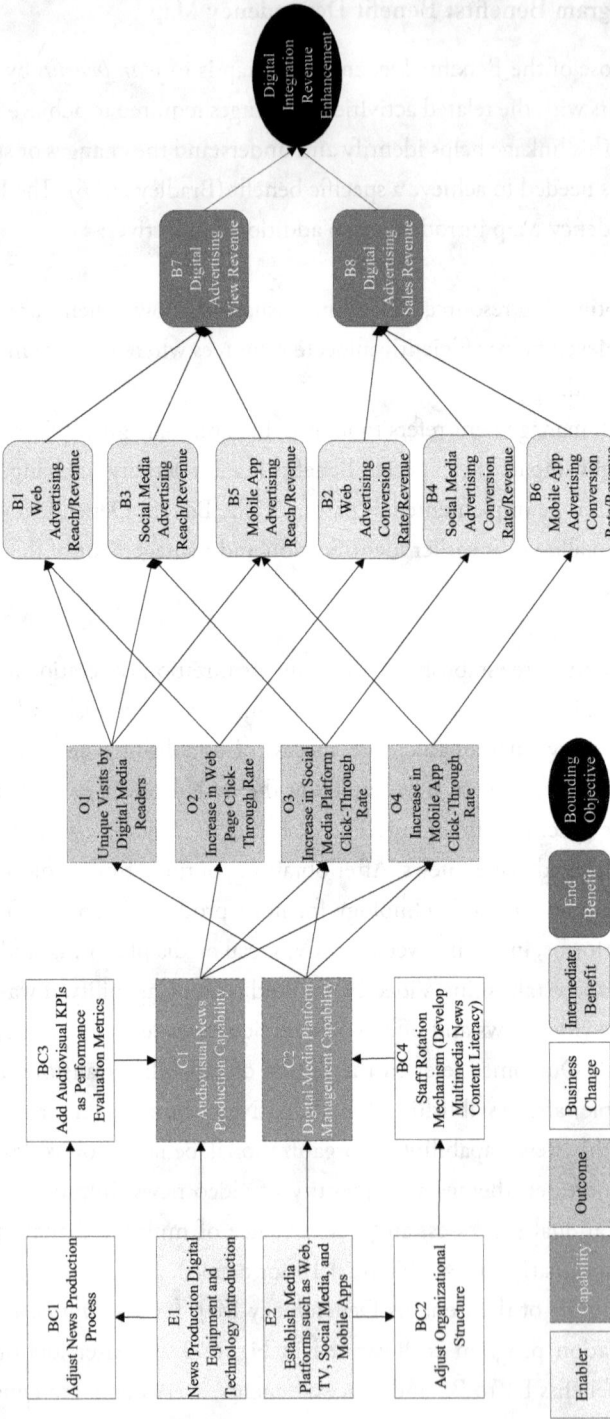

Figure 3.10 *The Benefit Dependence Map for The Sun News digital integration program*

how many projects are needed to achieve them. The outputs of projects E1 and E2 will create new organizational capabilities (C1 and C2). However, before these outputs can be transitioned to operational units and become the required capabilities (C1 and C2), business change activities BC1 and BC2 must be completed. Furthermore, even after acquiring new capabilities, the organization must undertake additional activities to transition these capabilities to operational units. For instance, BC3 and BC4 are necessary conditions for transitioning new capabilities to operational units, resulting in the change outcomes of O1, O2, O3, and O4. Ultimately, the outcomes O1, O2, O3, and O4 will enable the organization to achieve the process benefits B1 to B6.

Developing the Project Dossier

Purpose of the Project Dossier

The Project Dossier provides detailed information about the projects and activities that comprise the program, describing how executing these projects will deliver capabilities to the organization and outlining the anticipated outcomes and benefits of these projects. The purposes of designing the Project Dossier are:

- To avoid confusing interdependencies between projects.
- To provide a list of projects needed to achieve the Program Blueprint.

Content of the Project Dossier

The Project Dossier should include the following information for each project:

- Description of the project and its objectives
- Project requirements and their relationship to the Program Blueprint
- Specific outputs as required
- Time constraints for the project
- Dependencies on other projects
- Budget based on the Program Business Case
- Contribution to the program benefits

During the process of improving business operations, related projects and activities may undergo changes. All changes should be comprehensively evaluated based on timing, content, risks, and benefits.

As shown in Figure 3.11, the projects E1 and E2 in the benefit dependency map can be further subdivided into specific projects, which should be clearly defined in the project overview. For instance, as detailed in Table 3.3, E1 is broken down into the following projects: E1-1-1, Hardware Procurement and Installation Project for Studio, and E1-2, Software Procurement and Installation Project, among others. E2 is divided into two projects: E2-1 Cable TV Convergence Development Project and E2-2-1 Digital System Installation Project, including Digital Website Development.

Establishing Program Governance Arrangements

Governance Roles Within the Program Organization

Governance refers to the actions or processes of governing and managing an organization or system. In the context of benefit realization, it applies to the organization's investment in change. Governance is carried out by

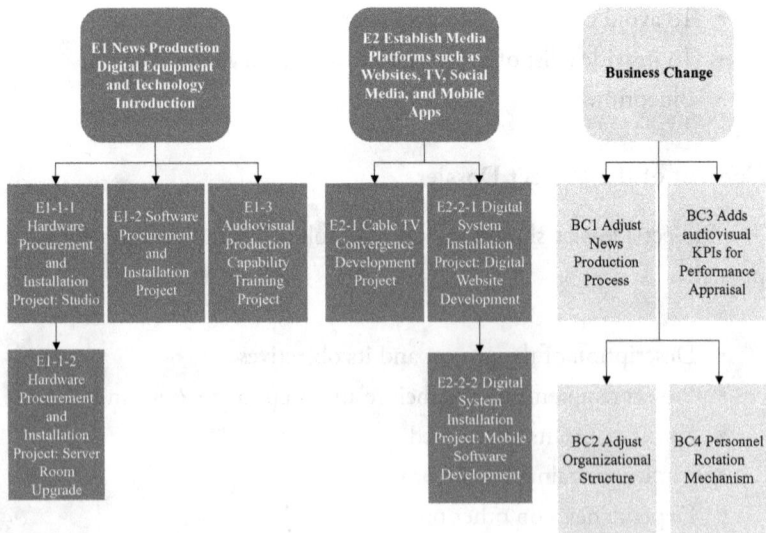

Figure 3.11 Project Dossier for The Sun News *digital integration program*

Table 3.3 *Project Dossier example for The Sun News digital integration program*

Project ID and title	Description	Resource requirements	Timetable and relationship with other projects	Budget (US$)	Major outputs and contributions
E1 News Production Digital Equipment and Technology Introduction					
E1-1-1 Hardware Procurement and Installation Project: Studio	The costs of building a photo booth include renovation as well as the purchase of photographic equipment, such as lighting, backdrops, cameras, lenses, and tripods.	• Purchase financing • Construction wage • Buildings	• Three months • Merged with E1-1-2 and E1-2 as the initial project to start	1 million	Professional Photo Studio
E1-1-2 Hardware Procurement and Installation Project: Server Room Upgrade	Importing or upgrading the equipment in the server room is required to maintain the digital system. Consider the design of the server room, including access control, network connections, and the installation of servers, routers, UPS systems, and other necessary equipment.	• Purchase financing • Construction wage • Buildings	• Three months • Merged with E1-1-1 and E1-2 to start the initial project	10,000 for the server. Data Storage Hard Disk 4.45/GB	Separate Server Room
E1-2 Software Procurement and Installation Projects	Import complete video and audio editing software	• Purchase financing • Maintenance wages	• Three months. • Started as an initial project at the same time as E1-1	80,000.	Complete video and audio editing software available for organization staff.

(continued)

Table 3.3 Project Dossier example for The Sun News *digital integration program (continued)*

Project ID and title	Description	Resource requirements	Timetable and relationship with other projects	Budget (US$)	Major outputs and contributions
E1-3 Audiovisual Production Capability Training Project	Invite professional audiovisual editors to conduct training on audiovisual production skills for existing media personnel.	• Training funding • Trainers • Training programs	• Six months • Continued after E1-2	Course 1,000/person	Enhance the performance of all staff in digital media production
E2 Establish Media Platforms such as Web, TV, Social Media Platforms, and Mobile Apps					
E2-1 Cable TV Convergence Development Project	One of the target convergence. Apart from equipment costs, this project will mainly involve staffing and channel costs.	• Broadcast slot fee • Production costs	• Three months • Continued after E1-1 and E1-2, combined with E2-2-1	Prices vary depending on the time of day chosen.	Developing one of the three converging streams
E2-2-1 Digital System Installation Project: Digital Website Development	One of the target convergence. Outsourcing the setup of the organization's website.	• Labor cost • Domain fee	• Two months • Continued after E1-1-2 and E1-2, merged with E2-1	Outsourcing: Initial website setup valued at 10,000–15,000	Developing one of the three converging streams
E2-2-2 Digital System Installation Project: Mobile Software Development	One of the target convergence. Outsourcing the development of an organization's mobile application software (APP).	• Labor cost • Development tools, hardware, and software equipment	• One month • Continued after E2-2-1	Outsourcing: The general business app development cost is between 10,000 and 25,000 per case.	Developing one of the three converging streams

Project ID and title	Description	Resource requirements	Timetable and relationship with other projects	Budget (US$)	Major outputs and contributions
Business Changes					
BC1 Adjusts News Production Process	Adjust the news production process to a more digital age model, increasing the production of audiovisual and interactive content.	• Professional consultant • IT team • Newsroom staff	Twelve months	1 million	Creating a more efficient and digital-ready news production process
BC2 Adjusts organizational structure	Created new organizational roles and established a business unit to manage the digital news production process better	• HR department • Leadership team • New role players	Six months	90,000	Implementation of a new organizational structure to support the required outcomes of digital convergence
BC3 Staff Rotation Mechanism	Enhancement of staff's multimedia news content quality	• HR department • Managers of the press department	Eighteen months	120,000	Enhance staff's multimedia content literacy to enable them to report more effectively in digital media.
BC4 Adds audiovisual KPIs for performance appraisal	Setting up audiovisual KPIs as the performance appraisal standard for employees.	• HR department • Management team • Professional consultant	Three months	30,000	Implemented a performance evaluation system based on AV KPIs to motivate staff to achieve Digital Convergence goals.

those who own or manage the funding, those likely to be affected by the change, or those who will derive the most value from the benefits. For a program, governance should be handled by affected stakeholders, such as the Program Governance Board, which is typically chaired by the Program Manager and is responsible for approving the release of funds and overseeing the achievement of expected benefits.

Elements of Program Governance

The elements of the Program Governance Plan include the following, with Table 3.4 providing an example of the Program Governance Plan for *The Sun News* digital integration program:

- Benefits management: Planning the benefits identification, prioritization, and delivery structure using the Benefit Profile and Benefits Realization Plan.
- Information management strategy: Planning how the program will catalog, document, store, and retrieve all information

Table 3.4 Program Governance Plan example for **The Sun News** *digital integration program*

Governance aspect	Governance plan
Benefits management	• The Program Manager: 1. Reports monthly to the Program Governance Board, tracking the actual progress of benefits as per the Benefit Map. 2. Reviews program status, organizational strategy, and external environment to assess whether adjustments are needed for achieving planned benefits.
Information management strategy	• The Program Manager assigns administrative staff from the Program Management Office to properly archive all data and documents produced by the program. • Relevant documents are primarily stored in digital format in a companywide encrypted database maintained by the IT department. • The Program Manager reviews data storage compliance weekly.

Governance aspect	Governance plan
Risk management strategy	• The Program Manager and Business Change Manager record potential risks for each phase of the program life cycle. • The Program Manager reviews the risk assessment and risk response matrix on a weekly basis to determine if updates are needed, while the Program Sponsor reviews these documents monthly.
Issue management strategy	• The Program Manager and Business Change Manager document potential issues for each phase of the program life cycle. • The Program Manager reviews the issue assessment table weekly to determine if updates are needed, while the Program Sponsor reviews these documents monthly.
Monitoring strategy	• The Program Manager and Business Change Manager review the current progress of the program weekly, monitoring project and activity execution to ensure alignment with expectations. • They formally report program progress to the Program Sponsor and Program Governance Board every month. • A semiannual review of program health is conducted, with the Program Manager reporting to the Program Governance Board.
Quality and assurance management strategy	• The Program Manager ensures that each project and business change activity within the program adheres to quality standards and has established inspection mechanisms. Monthly quality audits ensure project outcomes meet the defined quality standards.
Resource management strategy	• The Program Manager prepares a resource list detailing personnel, budget, hardware, and software and monitors resource needs and availability. • Records of used resources are maintained to provide accurate estimates of future program resource requirements.
Stakeholder engagement strategy	• The Program Manager creates a Stakeholder Profile, Power–Interest Matrix, and Stakeholder Map. • Four engagement strategies are planned based on the Stakeholder Profile: Close Communication, Keep Satisfied, Inform, and Monitor, as outlined in the stakeholder Power–Interest Matrix. • The Program Manager reviews and updates the Stakeholder Profile, Power–Interest Matrix, and Stakeholder Map every month.

through the Information Management Plan, outlining how to create and manage information.

- Risk management strategy: Planning how the program will establish risk identification, assessment, documentation, and contingency implementation.
- Issue management strategy: Planning how the program will uniformly manage issues arising throughout the program and handle any changes resulting from these issues.
- Monitoring and control strategy: Planning how the program will monitor progress toward expected outputs, outcomes, and key milestones, as well as the actual delivery progress through the Program Plan.
- Quality and assurance management strategy: Planning how to incorporate quality activities into program management through the Quality and Assurance Plan.
- Resource management strategy: Planning the resources consumed by the program, including financial, human, systems, facilities, and expertise, through the Resource Management Plan.
- Stakeholder engagement strategy: Planning who the stakeholders are, their interests and potential impacts, and how the program will engage them through the Stakeholder Profile and Communication Plan.

Developing the Program's Organizational Structure

Program Organizational Structure and Key Roles

Establishing a clear and effective organizational structure is crucial for the success of a program, ensuring that the program organization meets the needs of the program within its change context. Figure 3.12 shows the Program Organizational Structure. The responsibilities and tasks of the Sponsor Group, Program Manager, Program Governance Board, Program Manager, and Program Management Team were introduced in Chapter 2 of this book.

In addition to being overseen by the Business Change Manager, benefit realization within program management may also be the responsibility

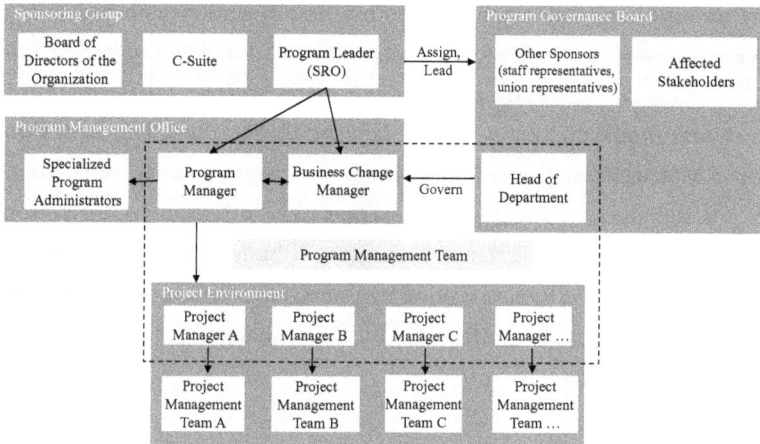

Figure 3.12 Program organizational structure diagram

of specific department heads directly affected by those benefits. These department heads will be responsible for maintaining the benefits. Below is an explanation of the Program Management Office and Business Change Manager, which have not yet been introduced in this book.

Program Management Office

The Program Management Office (PMO) serves as the nerve center and information hub for every program within the organization. All information, communication, monitoring, and control activities are coordinated through the PMO. The PMO has two distinct roles: providing support and guidance to projects and acting as a center for governance and control. Essential members of the PMO include Program Managers, Business Change Managers, and administrative staff, with the first two being complementary roles.

Business Change Manager

The Program Manager and Business Change Manager (BCM) have complementary roles: the former is responsible for delivering capability. At the same time, the latter is responsible for realizing the associated benefits by transitioning that capability into business operations and facilitating business changes to utilize the new capability. Suppose a program is implementing changes across different units of an organization. In that case, each unit should appoint a Business Change Manager to enhance the Program Management Team's understanding of specific business operations. When significant changes to business operations are required, the person appointed as Business Change Manager will be responsible for creating new business structures, operating methods, and working methods. The benefits may also directly affect the Business Change Manager (such as a department head).

Review and Approval of the Program Business Case

All documents in the Program Business Case, including the Program Blueprint, Benefit Profile, Benefit Dependency Map, Project Dossier, and Program Governance Arrangements, will be summarized and consolidated into a single document during the *Defining and Planning the Program* phase, ensuring stakeholders have access to all necessary information. The following four approval procedures are required to move forward:

- Approval by the Program Governance Board: Submit the complete documents to the Program Governance Board for approval and authorization.
- Endorsement by the Sponsoring Group: Seek formal endorsement from the program's Sponsoring Group to confirm that the program's design meets their expectations and requirements and to secure their commitment and support.
- Independent review: Conduct an independent assurance review to review the documents impartially.
- Authorization by the Program Manager to the Program Governance Board: The Program Manager must represent the organization to authorize and approve the continuation of the program, including committing the necessary resources.

The key tasks for the second phase, *Defining and Planning the Program,* are summarized as follows:

- The Program Manager prepares the Program Business Case by sequentially planning the program based on the Program Blueprint, Program Management Map, Project Dossier, Program Organizational Structure, and Program Governance Arrangements.
- The Program Blueprint describes the information needed to support operational practices, processes, and technologies in the future state, serving as the basis for planning the Program Management Map.
- The Program Management Map is developed sequentially from the Benefit Profile, Benefit Map, and Benefit Dependency Map. Throughout this process, the Program Manager must communicate frequently with stakeholders to identify all benefits and ensure that stakeholder expectations are met.
- Based on the Program Management Map, create a Project Dossier detailing the purpose, schedule, cost, and impact of each project within the program. This dossier is used to assess whether the planned projects are reasonable and capable of achieving the program's goals.
- Design the governance arrangements for the program to ensure that it is thoroughly considered and managed once it enters the execution and delivery phase.
- Consolidate the Program Business Case into a single document and submit it to the Program Governance Board for review and approval to proceed to the next phase, *Executing and Delivering the Program.*

Risk Considerations

During the Defining and Planning phase, risk and issue management transition from initial identification to structured and systemic handling. Risks at this stage often relate to blueprint ambiguity, benefit realization uncertainty, over-optimism in project interdependencies, or potential resistance to governance structures or business changes. Therefore, the decision to proceed to the next phase must be grounded in a clear understanding of the risk exposure surrounding the vision, blueprint, benefit map, and overall program plan.

A risk management strategy and issue management strategy should be developed and formally embedded into the program's governance arrangements. Such strategies define the principles, tools, and practices the program will use to identify, analyze, monitor, and control risks throughout the life cycle. An effective risk and issue management system provides essential support for this decision-making process, ensuring that both governance bodies and stakeholders are aware of the potential threats and mitigation paths before approving the continuation of the program.

A minimal system might include a spreadsheet to consolidate risk and issue entries outlined in the Program Brief and update during the development of the Program Blueprint, Benefit Profiles, and Project Dossier. Describe identified risks, note when they are most likely to surface, who should be responsible for controlling for each risk, and include a reference to any contingency plans, Such a document will serve as a dynamic repository to track potential and emerging risks—such as underestimated resource requirements, unrealistic benefit assumptions, interproject dependencies, or stakeholder misalignment—that could threaten the feasibility or integrity of the Program Business Case.

Checklist

Confirmation items	Check
• Completed the Program Blueprint	
• Completed the Program Business Case	
• Completed the Benefits Dependencies Map, and the identified business changes have been integrated into the Business Case	
• The comprehensive program planning has been reviewed and approved through the approval process	

Discussion Items

When considering the discussion questions, consider aspects of your organization or knowledge of project management to determine how a unique context (specific to your company) might influence your answer. How do these documents also inform the managers of the individual projects?

1. What does the Program Business Case include?
2. How are the benefits of the program identified, defined, and planned?
3. How is the Project Dossier produced?
4. What personnel and units are included in the program's organizational structure?
5. What is the purpose of establishing program governance, and what are the key components of the governance arrangements?

Complementary Reading

Bradley, G. 2016. *Benefit Realisation Management: A Practical Guide to Achieving Benefits Through Change.* CRC Press.

Fernandez, W., G. Klein, J. Jiang, and R. M. Khan. 2022. "Integration Networks in IT-Enabled Transformation Programs." *International Journal of Managing Projects in Business* 15 (6): 913–937.

Jiang, J. J., G. Klein, and W. D. Fernandez. 2018. "From Project Management to Program Management: An Invitation to Investigate Programs Where IT Plays a Significant Role." *Journal of the Association for Information Systems* 19 (1): 40–57.

Piney, C. 2017. *Earned Benefit Management: Aligning, Realizing, and Sustaining Strategy.* Auerbach Publications.

The Stationery Office. 2011 *Managing Successful Programmes (MSP).* 4th ed. AXELOS.

Wu, X., G. Klein, and J. J. Jiang. 2023. "On the Road to Digital Transformation: A Literature Review of IT-Enabled Program Management." *Project Management Journal* 54 (4): 409–427.

CHAPTER 4

Executing and Delivering the Program

After completing the second phase of defining and planning the program, the Program Sponsor and the governance board formally approve the Program Business Case, including the Program Blueprint, Program Management Map, Program Dossier, and Program Governance Arrangements. The board's approval marks the transition to the third phase of the program management life cycle: *Executing and Delivering the Program*. As shown in Figure 4.1, the Program Manager will begin executing the program based on the approved Business Case. This phase encompasses two major tasks:

1. Program control and capability delivery: This includes benefit realization management (BRM), establishing benefits measurement, and monitoring and controlling benefit realization. Activities related to realizing benefits will be iteratively conducted throughout each program phase.
2. Ongoing stakeholder communication: The goal is to keep stakeholders continuously updated and informed about the program's current status. Since programs often operate in environments with uncertain conditions and evolving requirements, ongoing communication with stakeholders ensures that the projects, program, and organization's strategic goals remain aligned.

Monitoring Program Delivery

The Program Manager must control all projects based on the benefits, project dependencies, schedules, and organizational structure defined in the previous phase, *Defining and Planning the Program* (e.g., ensuring projects are completed on time, monitoring benefit realization,

Phase III Prerequisites
1. Program Business Case

Phase III Main Tasks
1) Control and Deliver the Program
a) Managing the Benefit Realization
b) Delivering and Measuring the Benefits
c) Tracking and Monitoring the Benefits

2) Stakeholder Communication Management
a) Aligning Program Benefit Objectives with the Organization's Objectives
b) Aligning Project Deliverables with Program Benefit Objectives
c) Aligning Project Design with Program Benefit Objectives
d) Reviewing and Revising the Project Dossier

Governance Control
1. Oversight by the Program Governance Board
2. Accountability of the Program Manager to the Program Governance Board

Key Roles
1. Program Manager
2. Business Change Manager

Phase III Deliverable Document
1. Benefits Realization Tracking Report
2. Revised Project Dossier

Figure 4.1 Program execution and delivery

identifying potential risks, and handling project anomalies), and deliver new capabilities into business processes. The Program Manager should focus on tracking and controlling the realization of benefits. For benefit control and delivery, the Program Manager should:

- Use the performance indicators defined in the program's Benefit Profiles as the benchmark for benefits realization management.
- Track and measure actual benefit realization and assess the variance from target values.
- Continuously communicate with stakeholders about the status of any discrepancies and adjust projects based on change requests to ensure alignment with program, project, and organization's strategic goals.

Managing the Benefit Realization

BRM is crucial to the successful implementation of program management. The BRM framework spans phases to *Identify*, *Execute*, and *Sustain*, as shown in Figure 4.2.

Identify Benefits

This step involves identifying the benefits that are expected to be created to achieve the program's goals. This task is completed during the *Defining and Planning the Program* phase of the program management life cycle.

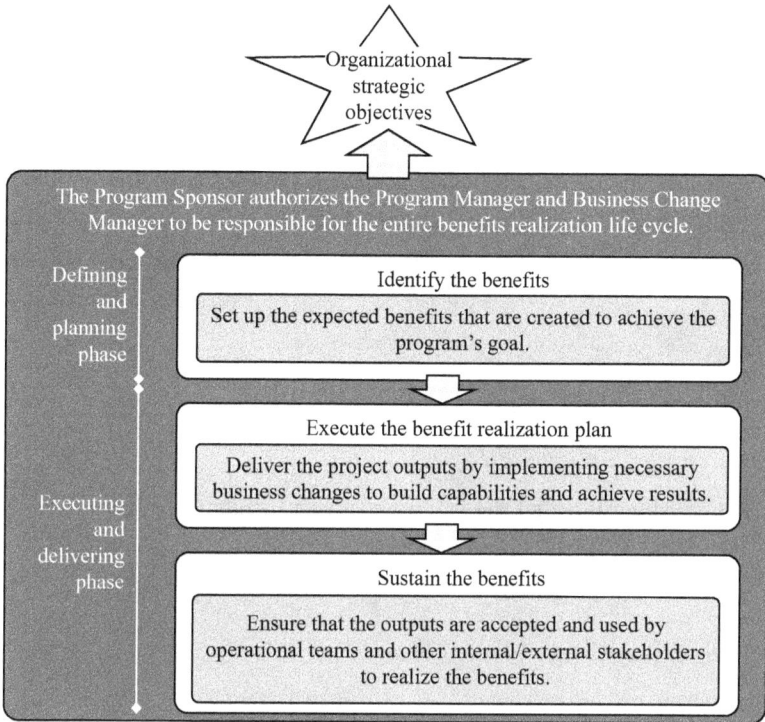

Figure 4.2 Benefit delivery life cycle

Execute the Benefit Realization Plan

In the program, this is an iterative and recursive process that continues until the benefits are realized. This process involves executing projects to build new organizational capabilities through project outputs, which are then applied in daily operations to produce results.

Sustain Benefits

This activity refers to the efforts of the Program Manager and Business Change Manager to realize and continuously deliver the benefits resulting from the program. Sustaining benefits is the final activity in benefit delivery, focusing on accepting and utilizing the results to achieve benefits. In the sustain phase, as benefits are continuously delivered into the organization's daily operations, the Business Change Manager must consider feedback and current conditions when adjusting the program's benefits.

The Program Manager utilizes benefits realization management to establish clear performance indicators for benefits, ensuring that the expected benefits contribute to achieving the organization's strategic objectives and provides benchmarks for tracking and controlling the delivery of benefits. This book previously covered benefits identification, definition, and planning during the *Defining and Planning the Program* phase (see Chapter 3, "Benefit Map, Benefit Profile, and Benefit Dependency Map"). This chapter will focus on delivering and measuring benefits, as well as tracking and monitoring them.

Benefits delivery and measurement:

- Execute the planned projects to achieve the expected benefits.
- Evaluate whether the program has successfully delivered the expected benefits.
- Analyze the gap between expected benefits and actual benefits.

Benefits tracking and monitoring:

- Regularly monitor the progress of benefits realization to ensure that the program remains on track and that benefits are realized as expected.
- Track benefit measurement indicators and compare actual performance with program goals.

Realizing benefits is a necessary condition for achieving program goals. It is essential to ensure that benefits are measured through relevant and reliable measurement processes defined in each Benefit Profile and overall benefits management. Each benefit requires identifying the baseline of the organization's current status and using the desired future state as the performance indicator for benefits realization, thus defining the measurement indicators for the benefit.

Depending on the program's objectives, various aspects of benefits should be measured, which largely depend on the program's nature, goals, and stakeholder expectations. The main aspects to consider include:

- Financial benefits: Cost savings, increased revenue, Return on Investment (ROI), Net Present Value (NPV), or cost–benefit ratios

- Operational benefits: Improved efficiency, reduced waste, increased productivity, and better resource utilization
- Strategic benefits: Alignment with organizational goals and strategies, competitive advantage, or market share growth
- Customer benefits: Increased customer satisfaction, enhanced customer loyalty, or improved customer experience

Delivering and Measuring Benefits

During the program's execution, stakeholders will mainly focus on the status of benefits delivery. Potential considerations for stakeholders include whether the Program Manager has accurately tracked all benefits, whether benefits realization has been monitored according to the specified measurement indicators, and whether benefits realization has been completed within the timelines outlined in the benefits realization management plan. To address these questions, the Program Manager must continuously track the achievement of each benefit. If delays beyond expectations are identified, further communication with stakeholders is required to identify potential issues and adjust the program design accordingly. In the worst-case scenario, if there is a significant discrepancy between the actual benefits realization and expected benefits within the timeline, consideration should be given to modifying or replacing the benefits.

Due to the various types of benefits and measurement indicators, benefits realization may occur either immediately or gradually. Based on the program's Benefit Profiles, the Program Manager must ensure that each benefit has clearly defined measurement indicators and performance targets before moving into iterative benefits delivery. For example, Figure 4.3 illustrates the Benefit Map developed during the Defining and Planning program phase.

The Benefit Map focuses on achieving the core benefits necessary for organizational change goals (i.e., financial benefits). However, during the execution of the program, when the realization of core benefits is progressing well, stakeholders may propose secondary benefits related to their affected interests as conditions for achieving the program's goals (e.g., operational benefits, strategic benefits, customer benefits).

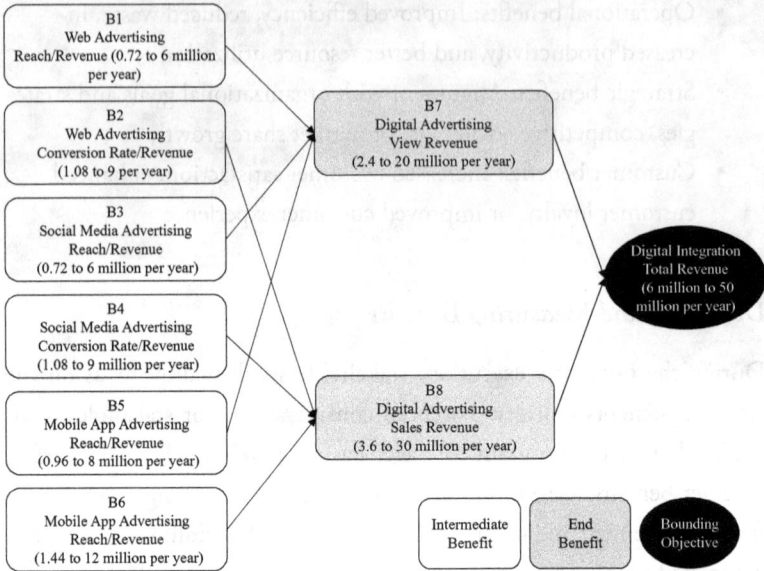

Figure 4.3 Benefit Map example for The Sun News *digital integration program*

Figure 4.4 illustrates three additional benefits for *The Sun News*: increased employee satisfaction, higher digitalization of work, and improved employee digital learning capabilities.

Based on the revised Benefit Map and its corresponding Benefit Profile, the Program Manager must track and monitor each benefit according to the measurement baseline values and benefit realization target values, as shown in Table 4.1. The measurement indicators must specify the performance levels required to achieve the target values. The newly recognized benefits are in the shaded cells of Table 4.1.

Additionally, beyond establishing metrics for benefits, including their baseline and target values, the performance of the program's goals should also be measured using appropriate indicators and target values. For example, in Figure 4.4, digital integration is the organizational strategy employed by *The Sun News*, and it is evaluated using four key indicators: social engagement, social influence, brand awareness, and brand reputation.

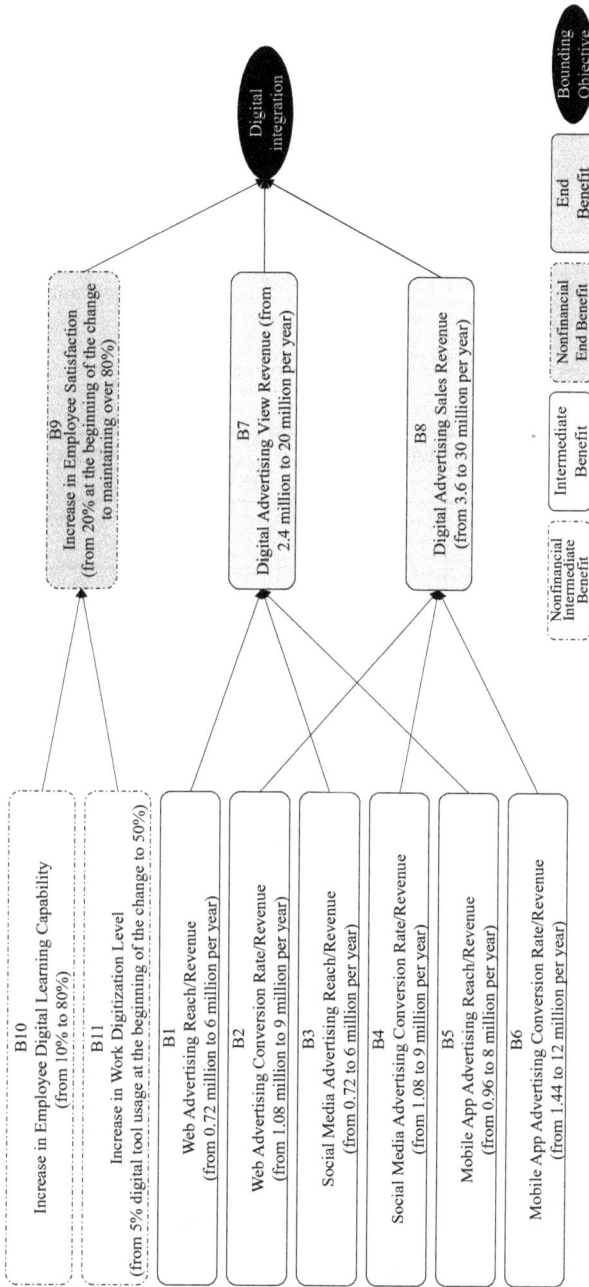

B9
Increase in Employee Satisfaction
(from 20% at the beginning of the change
to maintaining over 80%)

B7
Digital Advertising View Revenue (from
2.4 million to 20 million per year)

B8
Digital Advertising Sales Revenue
(from 3.6 to 30 million per year)

Digital
integration

B10
Increase in Employee Digital Learning Capability
(from 10% to 80%)

B11
Increase in Work Digitization Level
(from 5% digital tool usage at the beginning of the change to 50%)

B1
Web Advertising Reach/Revenue
(from 0.72 million to 6 million per year)

B2
Web Advertising Conversion Rate/Revenue
(from 1.08 million to 9 million per year)

B3
Social Media Advertising Reach/Revenue
(from 0.72 to 6 million per year)

B4
Social Media Advertising Conversion Rate/Revenue
(from 1.08 to 9 million per year)

B5
Mobile App Advertising Reach/Revenue
(from 0.96 to 8 million per year)

B6
Mobile App Advertising Conversion Rate/Revenue
(from 1.44 to 12 million per year)

Bounding
Objective

End
Benefit

Nonfinancial
End Benefit

Intermediate
Benefit

Nonfinancial
Intermediate
Benefit

Figure 4.4 Revised Program Benefit Map

Table 4.1 Benefits measurement indicators and performance metrics in the Program Benefit Profile

Benefit name	Baseline value (US$)	Target value (US$)
B1 Web Advertising Reach/Revenue	0.72 million/year	6 million/year
B2 Web Advertising Conversion Rate/Revenue	1.08 million/year	9 million/year
B3 Social Media Advertising Reach/ Revenue	0.72 million/year	6 million/year
B4 Social Media Advertising Conversion Rate/Revenue	1.08 million /year	9 million/year
B5 Mobile App Advertising Reach/Revenue	0.96 million/year	8 million/year
B6 Mobile App Advertising Conversion Rate/Revenue	1.44 million/year	12 million/year
B7 Digital Advertising View Revenue	2 million/year	20 million/year
B8 Digital Advertising Sales Revenue	4 million/year	30 million/year
B9 Increase in Employee Satisfaction	20% satisfaction at the start of the change	Monthly surveys to maintain over 80% satisfaction with the change
B10 Increase in Employee Digital Learning Capability	10% of employees pass the digital learning capability test at the start of the change	Quarterly tests with 80% of employees passing
B11 Increase in Work Digitization Level	5% of daily work completed using digital tools at the start of the change	Monthly surveys with 50% of daily work completed using digital tools

The indicators for the four digital integration strategic goals are explained as follows:

- Social engagement: Measure interaction data on major social media platforms, including the number of comments, shares, and likes. Additionally, observe interactions on the website, including reader comments, feedback, and participation.
- Social influence: Evaluate whether the reported issues spark social discussions, drive policy changes, or are cited by other media.

Also, the long-term social impact should be assessed, such as whether the reports help resolve social problems or shift public opinion.

- Brand awareness: Measure through market research, such as surveys asking respondents if they are aware of recent news reports by *The Sun News*. Check their search engine rankings and follower counts online on various social media platforms.
- Brand reputation: Assess through satisfaction surveys to gauge public trust in *The Sun News*. Brand reputation can also be evaluated based on ratings from professional agencies and awards or certifications received.

Tracking and Monitoring Benefits

Benefit realization involves managing all activities from the initial identification to achieving benefits. This activity involves monitoring project progress to ensure that outputs meet objectives and can be effectively integrated into operational units to achieve benefits. Benefit realization encompasses planning and managing the transition from old to new working methods while achieving outcomes that ensure operational stability and performance.

Tracking Benefit Realization Status

Monitoring is essential for recording performance and improving future outcomes. Similarly, tracking benefits helps to understand current performance and motivate improvement, as long as the measurements are appropriate and the goals are realistic. Tracking benefits focuses on the execution of the program and the progress of benefit realization. A key role of the Program Governance Board is to maintain the continuity of benefit realization. The Benefit Map helps determine the current status of benefits realization and allows continuous tracking to assess whether the overall program benefit realization is ahead or behind schedule. Basic steps include:

- Specify the benefits to be tracked based on the Benefit Map.
- Review the current performance indicators for these benefits, calculate the gap between current performance and target values, and report the results to relevant stakeholders.

- Mark benefits as achieved, not achieved, or overdue. Investigate overdue or potentially lagging benefits and develop corresponding response measures.

Using the Benefit Map to Report Benefit Realization Progress

During the benefit monitoring process, the Program Manager can use line charts based on clear indicators set for each benefit to track the degree of realization for all benefits. The Benefit Map can then be used to represent the progress of benefit realization in reports visually.

The Program Manager should regularly monitor benefit realization trends over the year. For instance, monitoring every two months allows for tracking whether all benefits are progressing as expected. In the case of *The Sun News*'s digital integration program, B7 and B8 are foundational for achieving the final benefits of the digital integration program. In the first year of implementation, B2 and B6 demonstrated significant progress, as illustrated in Figure 4.5. Typically, the Program Manager should present the overall benefit realization in the annual report using visual graphics to display the results of benefit tracking in the year following the program's execution. For example, Figures 4.6 through 4.10 show the status of benefit tracking after two and three years, indicating the extent to which each benefit has been achieved or remains to be achieved.

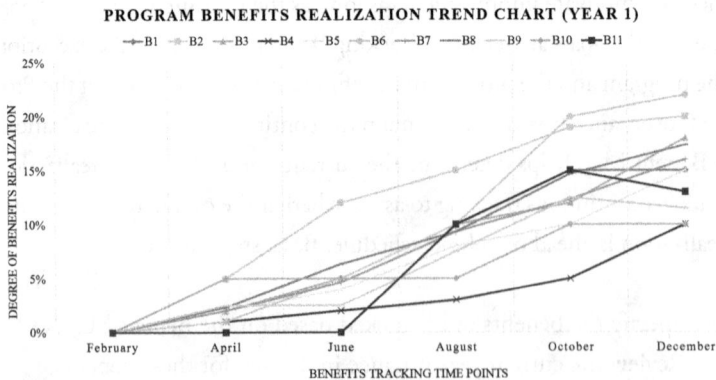

Figure 4.5 *Program benefits realization trend chart (first year of execution for* The Sun News's *digital integration program)*

Digital integration

B9
Increase in Employee Satisfaction (from 20% at the beginning of the change to maintaining over 80%)

B7
Digital Advertising View Revenue (from 2.4 to 20 million per year)

B8
Digital Advertising Sales Revenue (from 3.6 to 30 million per year)

B10
Increase in Employee Digital Learning Capability (From 10% to 80%)

B11
Increase in Work Digitization Level (From 5% digital tool usage at the beginning of the change to 50%)

B1
Web Advertising Reach/Revenue (From 0.72 million to 6 million per year)

B2
Web Advertising Conversion Rate/Revenue (From 1.08 million to 9 million per year)

B3
Social Media Advertising Reach/Revenue (From 0.72 to 6 million per year)

B4
Social Media Advertising Conversion Rate/Revenue (From 1.08 to 9 million per year)

B5
Mobile App Advertising Reach/Revenue (From 0.96 to 8 million per year)

B6
Mobile App Advertising Conversion Rate/Revenue (From 1.44 to 12 million per year)

Not Yet Due
Achieved
20% Remaining to Reach the Target
Exceeds Target Deadline

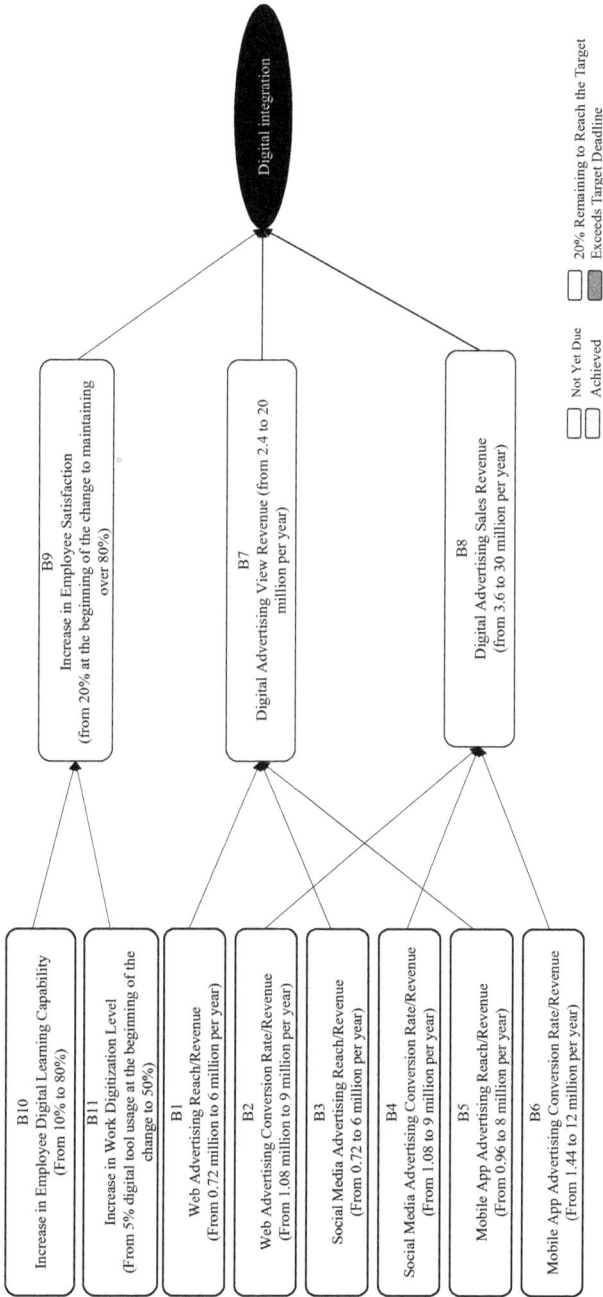

Figure 4.6 Benefits achievement status one year after The Sun News's digital integration program

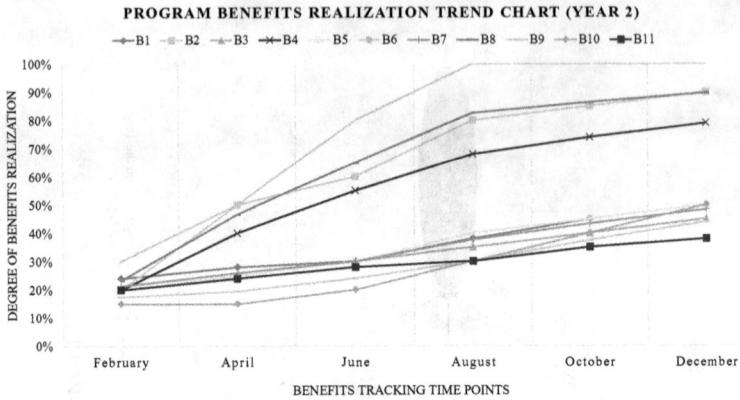

Figure 4.7 *Program benefits realization trend chart (second year of execution for* The Sun News's *digital integration program)*

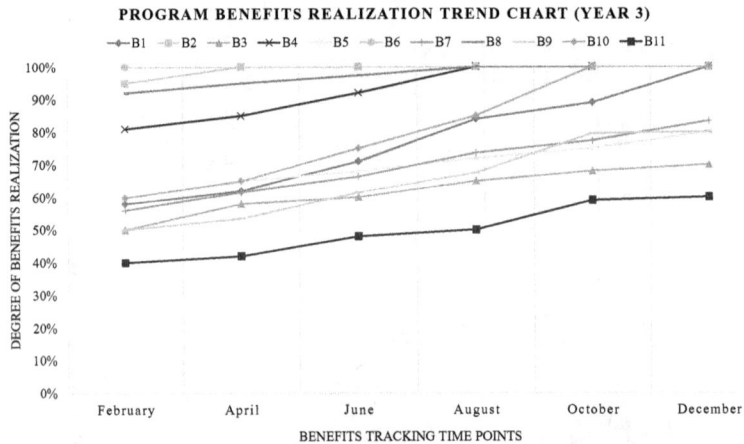

Figure 4.8 *Program benefits realization trend chart (third year of execution for* The Sun News's *digital integration program)*

Monitoring Benefit Realization

It is clear that, regardless of the program's duration, the Program Manager must regularly and continuously track the progress of benefit realization. The Program Manager should use tools such as the Program Business Case, Benefit Profile, and Benefit Dependency Map to monitor the progress of benefit realization, ensuring that the program maximizes potential improvements for the organization or minimizes the possibility of unrealized benefits.

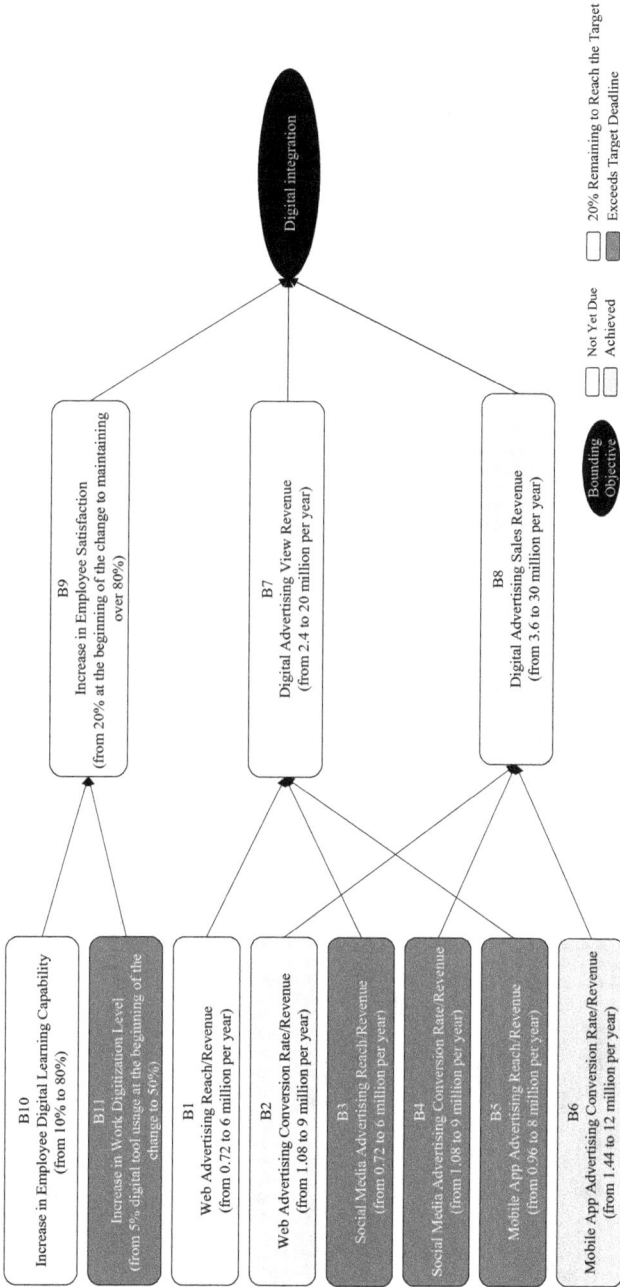

Figure 4.9 Benefits achievement status two years after the execution of The Sun News's digital integration program

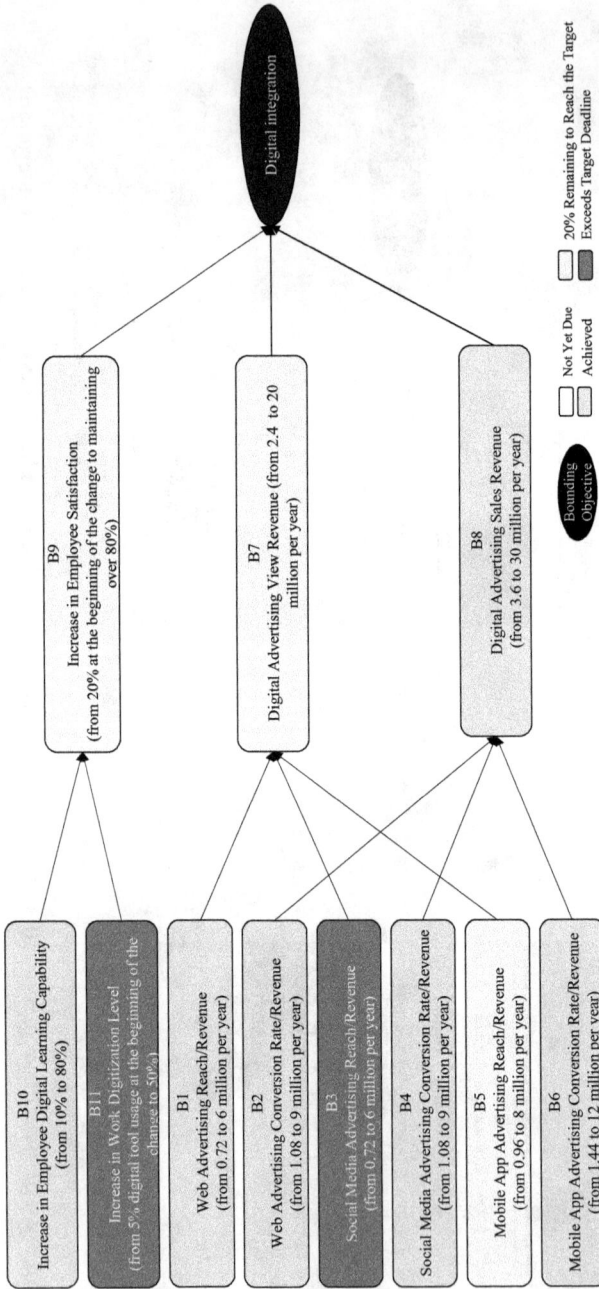

Figure 4.10 *Benefits achievement status three years after the execution of* The Sun News's *digital integration program*

However, during the monitoring process, challenges may arise, such as instability in business operations dependent on outputs from a specific project, changes in the external environment, or changes or repositioning of the program's goals. These factors can introduce variables affecting benefit realization. The Program Manager must communicate with stakeholders to reassess and adjust the Benefit Profile in response to the latest needs and organizational conditions.

Stakeholder Communication Management

Program Managers must maintain good communication with stakeholders, continuously track issues arising from environmental or stakeholder demand changes, and adjust benefit goals accordingly to ensure alignment between program design, project delivery, program benefit goals, and organizational strategy. Changes in the environment and demands are continuous, unpredictable, and inevitable during the implementation of a program. Many business managers describe VUCA, which is an acronym for four types of changing events: Volatility, Uncertainty, Complexity, and Ambiguity, as outlined in Figure 4.11, as the new normal for a chaotic and rapidly changing business environment in digital transformation programs.

An earlier discussion identified discrepancies that may occur between the achieved and targeted benefits. When the gap appears, the Program Manager must communicate with stakeholders to determine the reasons for delays in benefit realization and identify potential threats to the program's benefits. Continuous communication with stakeholders ensures that there is no information gap regarding the program's status and that the program's benefit goals remain aligned with the organizational strategy.

Aligning Program Benefit Goals with Organizational Strategy

When an organization's strategic goals change, the program's goals must also be adjusted. Since the purpose of setting program benefit goals is to achieve the organization's strategic goals, these changes

	VOLATILITY	UNCERTAINTY	COMPLEXITY	AMBIGUITY
Difficulty	Rapid and unexpected shifts	Lack of clarity about what will happen next	Many interconnected variables, hard to isolate cause and effect	No clear meaning or precedent
Information	Usually available, but may not indicate when or how change will happen	Available but often incomplete or contradictory	Abundant, but overwhelming or hard to interpret effectively	Lacking, irrelevant, or open to multiple interpretations
Causal relationship	Known, but the magnitude or frequency of change is unpredictable	Partially understood or ambiguous	Known in parts, but the full system impact is hard to model	Unknown or fundamentally unclear
Solutions or knowledge	Requires agile responses, buffers, and real-time adjustments	Scenario planning is needed	Requires systems thinking, simplification, and prioritization	Requires experimentation, reframing, and exploration
Predictability of outcome	Easier to predict the result	Harder to predict the result	Easier—the outcome may be known but is buried in noise	Harder—even the nature of the result is unknown
Understanding of change	Higher—understands what is changing, just not when or how fast	Higher—understands what is changing, but not what it means or leads to	Lower—too many interdependencies obscure what's changing	Lower—change lacks clarity in direction and nature

Figure 4.11 Characteristics of VUCA

will alter the Program Business Case, Benefit Map, and Benefit De-pendency Map. By updating the program's benefit goals, alignment with the organization's strategic objectives is maintained, ensuring the achievement of the organizational strategy. If the program becomes disconnected from the organizational strategy, it will be rendered ineffective.

In the case of *The Sun News* digital transformation, the initial goal of the digital integration program was to "present the media convergence trilogy, all centralized on screens: the first screen being traditional TV, the second screen being computers, and the third screen being mobile devices." With these three screens as final goals, a corresponding Benefit Map was designed. However, in the third year of execution, *The Sun News* began preparing a television channel. The Chief Operating Officer of the audiovisual division at the time stated,

> Due to the failure of the anticipated cable TV tiered payment system, the costs invested in the TV station by *The Sun News* could not be recovered. Additionally, with external environmen-tal changes, viewers shifted from cable TV to online platforms. Therefore, we decided to discontinue the TV channel and return to focusing on mobile device-based audiovisual services.

When the organization's strategic goals change, the expected benefit goals related to the television channel must be adjusted according to the new strategy and trends, shifting the focus to enhancing benefits related to mobile devices.

Aligning Project Deliverables with Program Benefit Goals

During the normal execution of a program, the Program Manager and Business Change Manager must ensure that the new capabilities deliv-ered by the project are transitioned into operational units and function properly. The Program Manager oversees the timely delivery of new ca-pabilities. In contrast, the Business Change Manager ensures the new ca-pabilities are integrated into daily operations and implements business changes to realize the corresponding benefits. This role distribution spans projects, programs, and organizational operational units, ensuring consistency between new capabilities delivered, program benefit goals, and their implementation within organizational operations.

The Business Change Manager focuses on three key aspects during the project delivery process:

- Determining daily business change needs and timelines ensures the new capabilities are smoothly integrated into business processes.
- Providing expertise from operational personnel and feedback to adjust the project accordingly.
- Ensuring that the operational status of new capabilities aligns with the program's benefit goals.

In the Program Business Case, the Program Manager has designed and planned the initial IT projects and business changes (revisit Chapter 3 for details). During the execution and delivery phase, if issues arise from integrating new capabilities into daily operations, similar adjustments (such as additions, deletions, or modifications) must be made to accommodate business changes.

In *The Sun News* digital transformation case, after the execution of initial IT projects (E1 and E2) and business changes (BC1 and BC2), the program delivered audiovisual news production capability (C1) and digital media platform management capability (C2) into daily operations. Once the staff had acquired the audiovisual news production capability, *The Sun News* planned further business changes, including adding audiovisual key performance indicators (KPI)s as performance evaluation metrics (BC3) and establishing a staff rotation mechanism (BC4). However, audiovisual news production capability could not be successfully implemented due to the independent actions of the editorial departments of *The Sun News*, *The Evening Sun*, and The Sun News Network. Consequently, an additional business change (BC5) was needed to integrate the editorial operations of *The Sun News*, *The Evening Sun*, and The Sun News Network, as shown in Figure 4.12.

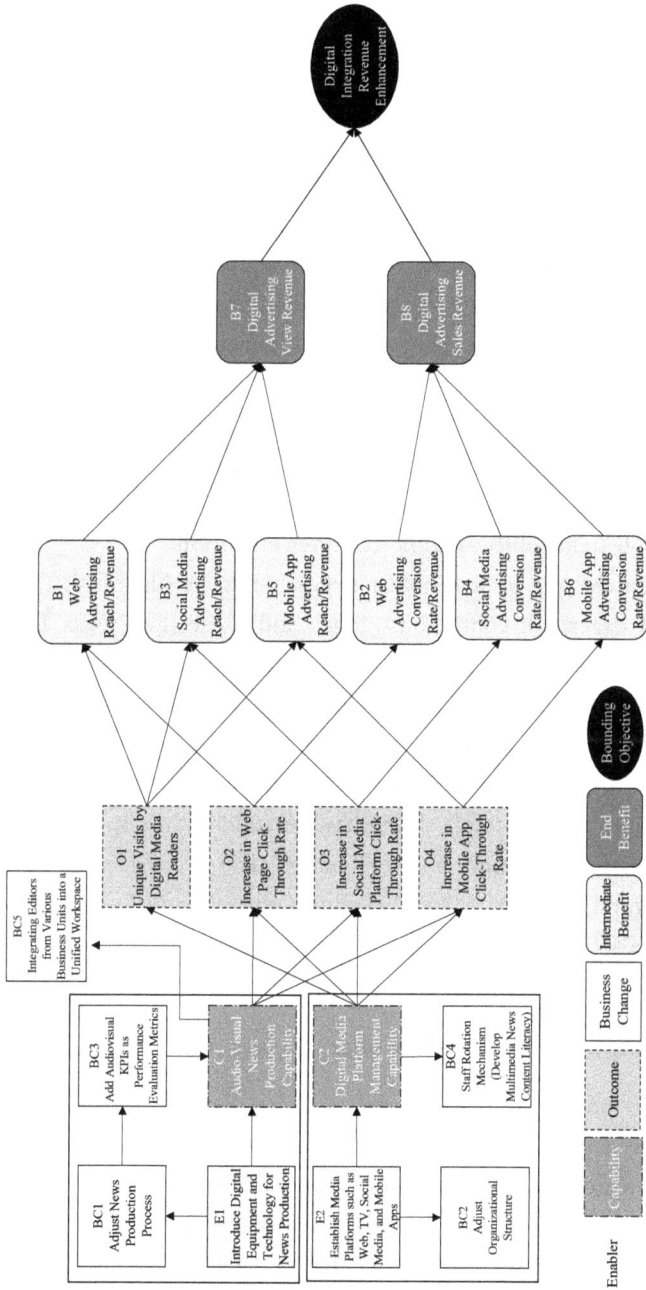

Figure 4.12 Revised Program Benefits Dependency Map

When new requirements are identified, the Program Manager will revise the preliminary Project Dossier prepared during the *Defining and Planning the Program* phase, as shown in Table 4.2.

Aligning Project Design with Program Benefit Objectives

In addition to potential adjustments to organizational strategy due to environmental changes, the program's execution may also be impacted by changes in stakeholder needs (e.g., changes in business operational needs). While monitoring the realization of program benefits, the Program Manager may find that a particular benefit is not being achieved as expected or that integrating new capabilities has led to new requirements. In such cases, the Program Manager must communicate with the benefiting stakeholders to understand the necessary additions, deletions, or adjustments required to align the project design with the program benefits objectives and continue execution.

When changes in stakeholder requirements are identified, the Program Manager will continuously track and revise the Project Dossier, making necessary additions, deletions, or modifications to the project design as needed. For instance, integrating audiovisual news production capabilities (C1) into daily operations has created new business demands that were not anticipated. As a result, an unforeseen business process integration project (BC5) has been added. In response to BC5, the program must include a new IT project (E3) to provide new business spaces and upgrade or provide relevant hardware facilities, as illustrated in Figure 4.13.

Reviewing and Revising the Project Dossier

Even if IT projects and business changes are well designed within the Program Business Case, adjustments to project design may still be necessary due to environmental or demand changes that occur during the benefit realization process. When the Program Manager identifies new requirements, the Project Dossier prepared during the *Defining and Planning the Program* phase will be revised, as shown in Table 4.2.

Table 4.2 *The revised Project Dossier of The Sun News digital integration program*

Project ID and title	Description	Resource requirements	Timetable and relationship with other projects	Budget (US$)	Major outputs and contributions
E1 News Production Digital Equipment and Technology Introduction					
E1-1-1 Hardware Procurement and Installation Project: Studio	The cost of building a photo booth includes renovation costs but also includes the purchase of photographic equipment, such as lighting, backdrops, cameras, lenses, and tripods	• Purchase financing • Construction wage • Buildings	• Three months Merged with E1-1-2 and E1-2 as the initial project to start	1 million	Professional Photo Studio
E1-1-2 Hardware Procurement and Installation Project: Server Room Upgrade	Importing or upgrading the equipment in the server room is required to maintain the digital system. Consider the design of the server room, including access control, network connections, and the installation of servers, routers, UPS units, and other necessary equipment.	• Purchase financing • Construction wage • Buildings	• Three months Merged with E1-1-1 and E1-2 to start the initial project	10,000 for the server. Data Storage Hard Disk 4.45/GB	Separate Server Room
E1-2 Software Procurement and Installation Projects	Import complete video and audio editing software	• Purchase financing • Maintenance wages	• Three months Started as an initial project at the same time as E1-1	80,000.	Complete video and audio editing software available for organization staff.

(continued)

Table 4.2 *The revised Project Dossier of The Sun News digital integration program (continued)*

Project ID and title	Description	Resource requirements	Timetable and relationship with other projects	Budget (US$)	Major outputs and contributions
E1-3 Training Program on Audiovisual Production Capability	Invite professional audiovisual editors to conduct training on audiovisual production skills for existing media personnel.	• Training funding • Trainers • Training programs	• Six months Continued after E1-2	Course 1,000/ person	Enhance the performance of all staff in digital media production
E2 Set Up Media Platforms such as Web, TV, Social Media Platforms, and Mobile Apps					
E2-1 Cable TV Convergence Development Project	One of the target convergence. Apart from equipment costs, this project will mainly involve staffing and channel costs.	• Broadcast Slot Fee • Production Costs	• Three months Continued after E1-1-1 and E1-2, combined with E2-2-1.	Prices vary depending on the time of day chosen	Developing one of the three converging streams
E2-2-1 Digital System Installation Project: Digital Website Development	One of the target convergence. Outsourcing the setup of the organization's website.	• Labor cost • Domain fee	• Two months Continued after E1-1-2 and E1-2, merged with E2-1	Outsourcing: Initial website setup valued at 10,000–15,000	Developing one of the three converging streams
E2-2-2 Digital System Building Project: Mobile Software Development	One of the target convergence. Outsourcing the development of an organization's mobile application software (APP).	• Labor cost • Development tools, hardware, and software equipment	• One month Continued after E2-2-1	Outsourcing: The general business app development cost is between 10,000 and 25,000 per case.	Developing one of the three converging streams

Project ID and title	Description	Resource requirements	Timetable and relationship with other projects	Budget (US$)	Major outputs and contributions
E3 Construction of Editing Space and Related Hardware Facilities	To meet the business integration needs of *The Sun News*, *The Evening Sun*, and The Sun News Network, this project involves outsourcing the redesign and construction of office spaces, including costs for design, painting, lighting, air conditioning, office furniture, computers, and communication equipment.	• Labor costs • Renovation costs • Basic equipment costs • Computer equipment costs	• One month Executed before the BC5 business change process	Outsourced: Pricing based on requirements, evaluated and quoted by a professional renovation company	Supports the establishment of a new business structure
Business Changes					
BC1 Adjusts News Production Process	Adjust the news production process to a more digital age model, increasing the production of audiovisual and interactive content.	• Professional consultant • IT team • Newsroom staff	Twelve months	1 million	Creating a more efficient and digital-ready news production process

(continued)

Table 4.2 *The revised Project Dossier of The Sun News digital integration program (continued)*

Project ID and title	Description	Resource requirements	Timetable and relationship with other projects	Budget (US$)	Major outputs and contributions
BC2 Adjusts organizational structure	Created new organizational roles and established a business unit to manage the digital news production process better	• HR department • Leadership team • New role players	Six months	90,000	Implementation of a new organizational structure to support the required outcomes of digital convergence
BC3 Adds audiovisual KPIs for performance appraisal	Setting up audiovisual KPIs as the performance appraisal standard for employees.	• HR department • Management team • Professional consultant	Three months	120,000	Implemented a performance evaluation system based on AV KPIs to motivate staff to achieve Digital Convergence goals better.
BC4 Staff Rotation Mechanism	Enhancement of staff's multimedia news content quality	• HR department • Managers of the press department	Eighteen months	200,000	Enhance staff's multimedia content literacy to enable them to report more effectively in digital media
BC5 Integration of Editors from Various Business Units into a Unified Workspace to Enhance Coordination and Collaboration	Establish a large-scale editorial workspace and design a new editorial workflow to improve resource integration across business units' news production process.	• HR department • Leadership team • Workspace	Six months	1 million	Implementation of a new workspace layout to support collaboration and coordination among business units for digital integration

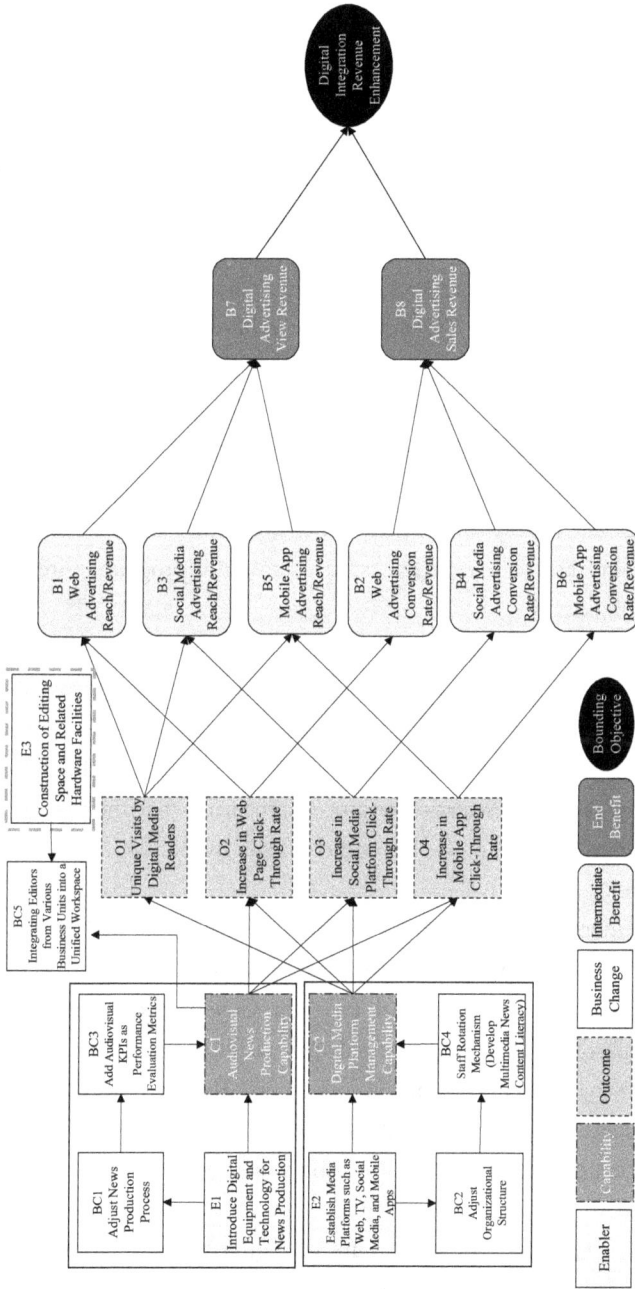

Figure 4.13 Revised Program Benefits Dependency Map based on requirements

Risk Considerations

As the program enters the execution and delivery phase, risk and issue management move from strategic planning to active operational control. Here, the program begins to implement the governance plan defined in the previous phase. Managing risks and issues is no longer theoretical—it becomes a continuous and dynamic part of delivering benefits, controlling project tranches, and sustaining alignment with the organization's strategic objectives.

Each major advance of program activity brings a new layer of complexity, uncertainty, and dependency, especially as benefit realization begins. The Program Manager must proactively monitor for early warning signs that indicate risk exposure, such as delays in capability deployment, variances in benefit indicators, stakeholder dissatisfaction, or shifting external conditions. As outlined in the Benefit Dependency Map and Project Dossier, these interdependencies mean that risks in one project or capability area can rapidly cascade across the program, threatening broader objectives.

Programs must also manage aggregated risk exposure, recognizing that the cumulative impact of multiple low-level risks across several projects can be more damaging than any single isolated issue. Therefore, project teams are expected to escalate risks and issues in accordance with clear cross-program escalation protocols, ensuring that the program remains aware of any factors that could impact overall delivery or benefit realization.

To support this, risk and issue documentation should be actively maintained, with updates reviewed regularly by the Program Manager, Business Change Manager, and Program Governance Board. Leaving issues unresolved or undocumented may result in misalignment, stakeholder disengagement, or unrealized benefits. The program should regularly evaluate the effectiveness of its risk and issue management processes during each review, adjusting mitigation strategies or escalation pathways as needed.

Finally, given the VUCA nature of digital transformation environments, the program must remain flexible and responsive. Triggers such as evolving stakeholder needs, shifting strategic goals, or misaligned capability integration must be treated not as isolated deviations but as signals for proactive adjustment. Robust risk management is therefore essential—not only to protect the program's execution but also to preserve its strategic value and long-term benefits.

The following checklist provides a summary of the activities conducted in the *Executing and Delivering the Program* phase.

Checklist

Confirmation items	Check
• Is communication with stakeholders in line with the approved Program Communication Plan, and is it effective? Are there continuous communications with relevant stakeholders throughout the execution process?	
• Is there sufficient infrastructure in place to ensure effective program governance?	
• Are the development, delivery, and application of new capabilities proceeding as outlined in the program plan?	
• Is there adequate monitoring of the external environment and significant internal changes that might impact the organization and necessitate strategic adjustments?	
• Is the change being implemented according to the program plan?	
• Are there sufficient contingency measures in place to address uncertainty and risks during the program's execution?	
• Is there a rolling deployment based on benefits (e.g., iterative modifications to the Business Case)?	
• Are the benefits being realized as expected? Are corrective or adjustment measures being taken if the goals are not met?	
• Regularly review the project team to assess their relationship with the program, including: ○ How does your project output contribute to organizational change? ○ What benefits does your project output deliver? ○ What new capabilities does your project output build for the organization to achieve benefits? ○ Are there other projects that are dependent on your project to deliver the expected output? ○ What benefits are affected by the outputs of these other projects? ○ What is the current status of these other projects?	

Discussion Items

Delve deeply into the questions below, drawing on your knowledge and experiences. Look for practices that are similar to those in your current organization. How do stakeholders and communication with stakeholders differ between projects and programs?

1. What is the life cycle of BRM?
2. What are the steps to track the status of benefit realization?
3. Why is it necessary to maintain communication with stakeholders?
4. Under what circumstances should the content of the Project Dossier be added, removed, or modified?

Complementary Reading

Bennett, N., and J. Lemoine. 2014. "What VUCA Really Means for You." *Harvard Business Review* 92 (1/2): 27.

Bradley, G. 2016. *Benefit Realisation Management: A Practical Guide to Achieving Benefits Through Change.* CRC Press.

Piney, C. 2017. *Earned Benefit Management: Aligning, Realizing, and Sustaining Strategy.* Auerbach Publications.

PMI (Project Management Institute). 2017. *The Standard for Program Management.*4th ed. PMI.

PMI (Project Management Institute). 2018. *Benefits Realization Management: A Practice Guide.* PMI.

The Stationery Office. 2011. *Managing Successful Programmes (MSP).* 4th ed. AXELOS.

Tsai, J. C. A., X. Wu, G. Klein, and J. J. Jiang. 2022. "Goal Equivocality and Joint Account of Meaning Creation in an Enterprise System Program." *Information Systems Management* 39 (1): 82–97.

Wu, X., G. Klein, and J. J. Jiang. 2023. "On the Road to Digital Transformation: A Literature Review of IT-Enabled Program Management." *Project Management Journal* 54 (4): 409–427.

CHAPTER 5

Closing the Program

The program should be closed when it achieves the anticipated benefits or if environmental changes make it unworthy to continue. Given the substantial resources consumed from the program's start to its end, it is crucial to audit the program to accurately measure its costs and benefits for a fruitful analysis of performance and resulting capabilities. Furthermore, an organization must preserve and transfer the experience gained during the process to meet the need for continual improvement in its program management processes. This transfer of knowledge helps build the organization's capacity to manage programs and achieve organizational change. With those purposes in sight, the fourth phase of the program management life cycle considers when a program should be closed, the conditions for closure, and closing activities (Figure 5.1).

Closing the Program

Programs typically last for extended periods, sometimes for several years. If a program is left floating indefinitely and treated as a regular part of business, it poses risks to the organization. Thus, the program closure

Phase IV Prerequisites
1) Program Benefit Realization

Governance Control
1. Program Governance Board Authorization
2. Closure Process Review

Key Roles
1. Program Senior Responsible Owner (SRO)

Phase IV Main Tasks
1) Closing the Program
2) Reviewing the Program
3) Updating and Archiving the Program Information
4) Disbanding the Program
5) Lessons Learned Feedback

2. Program Governance Board
3. Program Manager
4. Business Change Manager
5. Program Management Office

Phase IV Deliverable Document
1. Updated Program Documentation
2. Program Lessons Learned Report
3. Oversight Arrangements for Remaining Activities

Figure 5.1 Program closure activities

phase aims to ensure that the program's final objectives are formally acknowledged as having been completed. This activity indicates that the program has successfully delivered the new capabilities described in the Program Blueprint and assessed their outcomes through benefit measurement. Some benefits may have been realized during the program's execution, while others might only be fully realized after completing the final project.

Closing a program involves evaluating the benefits achieved to date. If significant time is required to continue benefit realization activities after capability delivery, maintaining the entire program management structure to control these final activities is impractical. It might be necessary to manage these benefit realization activities as a separate project after the program's closure.

Thus, program closure includes a final evaluation of the program and the release of its resources and infrastructure. Program closure can be scheduled after the final project in the Program Dossier is completed and the required capabilities are delivered. The exact timing of formal program closure will depend on the support needed to ensure the new operational environment is fully transitioned to the operational units. In addition, any unresolved (incomplete) benefit realization activities should be evaluated to determine whether the entire program infrastructure needs to remain in place or can be reduced to simple monitoring and reporting.

Key Points for Program Closure

- All activities planned in the Program Blueprint have been delivered.
- The benefits have been realized.
- The Program Business Case has been satisfied.
- Realized benefits can be maintained.
- Final project deliverables have been completed according to the Program Plan.
- No outstanding risks or issues that could adversely impact daily operations.

Signs That a Program Should Be Closed Early

- Evidence suggests that the program lacks business value and cannot be sufficiently adjusted to produce an acceptable Program Business Case.
- The organization lacks sufficient funding and resources to complete the remaining work.
- Significant external changes have made the remaining aspects of the program irrelevant.
- The organization has changed its strategy for internal reasons rather than due to external environmental changes, making the program invalid.
- The remaining costs of completing the program outweigh the additional benefits that would be realized.

Reviewing the Program

During the program, evaluations at the end of each phase monitor and assess benefit realization. As part of program closure, a formal review should be conducted to assess the delivery of the complete Program Blueprint, the realization of overall benefits, and the achievement of the Program Business Case. Benefit evaluations should have been carried out during the execution and delivery phases so the final review focuses on the comprehensive results post-benefit realization. The closure review process should also evaluate the overall performance and management of the program to identify lessons learned that can be applied to future programs (e.g., team composition, estimation methods, intelligence gathering techniques).

Updating and Archiving Program Documentation

In addition to reviewing performance during the program's execution, it is essential to review related documents, such as strategies and program plans, to assess their effectiveness, appropriateness, and the learning experience for future programs. The documentation scope should encompass all information that impacts business and legal regulatory requirements.

Furthermore, program documents (including the Program Blueprint, Program Business Case, Program Dossier, and Benefit Profile) should be reviewed and updated to ensure that any remaining issues, risks, and incomplete actions are appropriately addressed and handed over to the operational departments responsible for managing these issues. It is important to note that responsibility for these risks and issues remains with the Program Manager.

After the review, feedback should be provided to strategists (typically the organization's board or top executives) for programs initiated to achieve strategic goals. No strategy guarantees success, but positive feedback from the program will help the organization make more informed and better strategic decisions.

Disbanding the Program

After completing the above processes in the program closure phase, the program's infrastructure and management units should be dissolved, and the personnel and resources involved in the program should be released to other projects, programs, or operations. Before dissolution, staff reallocation within the organization should be planned. Employees will have gained enhanced skills from their experience in the program, which will be reflected in their future career development. These employees are most likely valuable resources, and every reasonable consideration should be taken to retain them for the organization's future.

Any contracts used by the program should be finalized and concluded, or the responsibility for ongoing contract management should be transferred to the relevant business management units.

Lessons Learned Feedback

A program is a learning organization that continuously examines and enhances its performance throughout its life cycle. Programs tend to perform more effectively when management members adopt a learning-oriented mindset. The program team is regularly adjusted and adapted to achieve this based on accumulated experience and ongoing results. This reflective approach necessitates built-in adjustments at key review points, allowing the management team and individual members to assimilate insights and apply them as the program evolves. Consequently, in the closing phase— or even at the end of each phase—the effectiveness of learning from experience can be evaluated by assessing the quality of review processes, the extent to which lessons from past changes are applied, and their impact on both the program and the business performance metrics used to measure internal effectiveness.

Furthermore, the program board must ensure that the program aligns with strategic objectives and should actively support the review processes, assimilate lessons learned, and drive continuous performance improvements. Knowledge gained should be documented and made systematically available (e.g., a central PMO, an organizational knowledge management system).

Since programs are often initiated to achieve corporate strategic goals, they must provide meaningful feedback to strategic decision makers. No strategy is guaranteed to succeed, but high-quality feedback from each program enables the organization to make more informed and effective strategic decisions.

Risk Considerations

Effective program closure not only marks the end of program execution but also serves as the final checkpoint for validating that all strategic objectives, capabilities, and benefits have been delivered, sustained, or transitioned appropriately. From a risk management perspective, this phase is crucial to prevent latent risks from undermining long-term benefit realization or daily operations after the program has concluded.

Prior to formal closure, the program's risk and issue management strategies must be reviewed and updated one final time. The Program Manager is responsible for confirming that there are no outstanding risks or unresolved issues that could negatively impact operational performance. If any such items remain, they must be documented, accompanied by mitigation plans, and formally handed over to the responsible operational units.

Programs may also face premature closure. In such cases, risk and issue management play a central role in evaluating the program's viability. A program that can no longer deliver acceptable outputs, outcomes, or benefits—whether due to unresolvable internal challenges or major external shifts—must be assessed pragmatically. Escalating risks such as strategic misalignment, budget shortfalls, or systemic capability failure must trigger serious consideration of early termination. When this occurs, risk and issue planning should inform both the closure decision and the contingency planning needed to wind down the program responsibly.

Regardless of whether the program closes successfully or prematurely, completing the risk management cycle is essential. Documents must be finalized, responsibilities reassigned, and all governance documents (e.g., Program Blueprint, Business Case, Benefit Profile) updated to reflect the final status of risks and issues. Lessons learned in risk handling—particularly from escalations, mitigations, and cross-project interdependencies—should be explicitly documented as part of the program review, helping future programs to avoid similar pitfalls. Through disciplined closure and risk finalization, the organization not only protects its investments but also enhances strategic learning and resilience in future transformation initiatives.

Discussion Items

1. Under what conditions can a program be closed? How should an organization learn from closing decisions?
2. What must be confirmed to close a program formally? What metrics would you recommend to measure financial performance?
3. What is the purpose of reviewing the program?
4. What is the purpose of updating and archiving program documentation? Other than future program managers, who can benefit from an analysis of the program's performance (and how)?
5. How should incomplete benefits and program-related personnel be managed when dissolving the program?

Complementary Reading

Bradley, G. 2016. *Benefit Realisation Management: A Practical Guide to Achieving Benefits Through Change.* CRC Press.

Jiang, J., G. Klein, and W. Huang. 2020. *Projects, Programs, and Portfolios in Strategic Organizational Transformation.* Business Expert Press.

Piney, C. 2017. *Earned Benefit Management: Aligning, Realizing, and Sustaining Strategy.* Auerbach Publications.

PMI (Project Management Institute). 2017. *The Standard for Program Management.* 4th ed. PMI.

The Stationery Office. 2011. *Managing Successful Programmes (MSP).* 4th ed. AXELOS.

Tsai, J. C. A., X. Wu, G. Klein, and J. J. Jiang. 2022. "Goal Equivocality and Joint Account of Meaning Creation in an Enterprise System Program." *Information Systems Management* 39 (1): 82–97.

Wu, X., G. Klein, and J. J. Jiang. 2023. "On the Road to Digital Transformation: A Literature Review of IT-Enabled Program Management." *Project Management Journal* 54 (4): 409–427.

CHAPTER 6

Conclusion

We conclude by summarizing the concepts and dominant tools presented in Chapters 1 through 5. Furthermore, we examine concerns related to culture and the importance of managing change within the organization.

Chapter Summaries

Chapter 1—Digital Transformation and IT-Enabled Program Management

Chapter 1 discusses how digital programs can achieve organizational digital strategic goals and how real-time feedback from the operational layer can be used to adjust strategies. The IT-enabled program life cycle is divided into four phases: Identification and Formulation, Definition and Planning, Execution and Delivery, and Closure. The primary focus of the *Identification and Formulation* phase includes two key aspects: strategic (value) decision management and stakeholder analysis. The *Definition and Planning* phase emphasizes goal management, program documentation design, and allocation of organizational and personnel resources. The *Execution and Delivery* phase involves monitoring, delivering IT capabilities, and realizing the benefits of IT. The *Closure* phase includes reviewing the realization of benefits and analyzing the experiences gained during execution. The chapter further introduces the five main principles of program management, the three core responsibilities, and the five key skills of the IT-enabled Program Manager. Finally, it reminds readers to understand the applicability of various situations, maintain a dynamic work approach, continuously gather information to stay current with market changes and ensure that their knowledge remains up-to-date.

Chapter 2—Identifying and Formulating the Program

Chapter 2 introduces the first phase of the program life cycle, *Identifying and Formulating the Program*. This phase is divided into two tasks: (1) Identifying the Pre-program and (2) Establishing the Program. During the identification of the pre-program, after understanding the threats or opportunities brought by environmental changes, the Program Sponsor can begin drafting the program vision in the early phases, discussing it with key stakeholders to seek resource sponsorship, and forming a sponsorship team. The sponsorship team then appoints a Program Manager to initiate the program life cycle, assigning them to establish a program management team for preliminary planning. Tasks include creating an Organizational Strategy Map, identifying and analyzing stakeholders, and ultimately completing the Program Vision Statement to achieve consensus among all stakeholders on the future state.

In the program formulation phase, the Program Strategy Map is created, a Program Mandate is developed, and the program management team's purpose, scope, cost, responsibilities, and authorities are defined. The Program Brief is then prepared, expanding on the Program Mandate and analyzing the program's feasibility in detail. The Program Preparation Plan is developed, reviewed, and approved internally to secure resources for program execution. This chapter uses *The Sun News* case as a template, providing examples of the various steps to help readers understand practical applications.

Chapter 3—Defining and Planning the Program

Chapter 3 introduces the second phase of the program life cycle, *Defining and Planning the Program*. This phase begins with the production of a Program Business Case to help evaluate whether the program has sufficient value. This evaluation employs a Program Blueprint that illustrates the specific outcomes the project can bring, highlighting the differences between the current state and the future state. The tool identifies, defines, and plans program benefits, creating a Benefit Map and a Benefits Dependency Map. After completing the benefits planning, a Project Dossier is designed, which provides a detailed description of the planning and objectives of each project within the program, as well as its requirements. Finally, the chapter introduces the program's organizational structure, with a focus on program governance activities.

Chapter 4—Executing and Delivering the Program

Chapter 4 introduces the third phase of the program life cycle, *Executing and Delivering the Program*. This phase requires controlling the program and delivering capabilities iteratively to realize benefits. It emphasizes continuous communication with stakeholders to inform them about the program's status. The primary purpose of program control and delivery is to measure and evaluate benefit realization, utilizing BRM (benefits realization management) to establish clear benefit performance indicators that aid in assessment. When monitoring benefits, progress can be visualized to track the current status. When adding, removing, or adjusting program benefits and projects, it is essential to ensure that the program's objectives and requirements remain aligned with the organizational strategic direction.

Chapter 5—Closing the Program

Chapter 5 introduces the final phase of the program life cycle, *Closing the Program*. Closing the program indicates that the expected benefits have been realized or that the program can no longer continue due to environmental or fiscal changes. During closure, it is essential to document the costs, resources, and all planning records utilized in the program, preserving all experiences and knowledge gained as valuable assets for the organization. If the program is formally closed, it is necessary to ensure that the Business Case is satisfied, all projects are completed, and the remaining activities are successfully transferred to other units. The entire period of benefit realization should be reviewed, and strategic and planning information should be updated and archived internally for future reference. Finally, the program team and units should be disbanded, personnel reassigned within the organization, and resources released.

Culture–Technology View in the IT-Enabled Program

The actual execution of program management encompasses two dimensions: technological and cultural aspects, as illustrated in Figure 6.1. Together, these two dimensions form the framework for program management, mutually influencing each other and jointly determining the program's success.

Technological Dimension

The technological dimension includes strategy and program identification, definition and planning, execution and delivery, risk management, and progress monitoring. A clear Program Mandate outlines the program's vision, scope, expected budget, and timeline. The Program Brief links the feasibility assessment, defining the program's objectives, expected benefits, potential risks, cost estimates, and schedule. The Program Preparation Plan is used to plan the Program Governance Arrangements, resources, and anticipated timeline. The Program Business Case confirms the program's scope, direction, and objectives and outlines the specific execution methods and tasks. Finally, BRM serves as a method for tracking and monitoring, evaluating the program's overall progress through the realization of benefits. A successful Program Manager will be well trained in the technological dimension of program management.

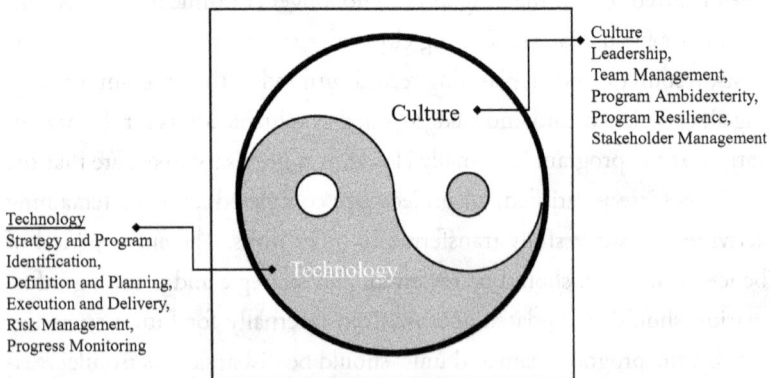

Culture
Leadership,
Team Management,
Program Ambidexterity,
Program Resilience,
Stakeholder Management

Culture

Technology
Strategy and Program
Identification,
Definition and Planning,
Execution and Delivery,
Risk Management,
Progress Monitoring

Technology

Figure 6.1 Cultural and technological dimensions of IT-enabled program management

Cultural Dimension

The second dimension, which contrasts with the technological dimension, is the cultural dimension of program management. Unlike the orderly world of program planning, this dimension involves a more chaotic, often conflicting, and contradictory environment during execution. It focuses on establishing temporary social systems within a larger organizational environment that combines various expertise to complete the program. The Program Manager must cultivate a program culture that promotes teamwork and stakeholder engagement while also fostering the ability to identify and resolve issues that threaten the program promptly.

In practice, things rarely go as planned, so the Program Manager must be capable of leading the program back on track or adjusting the execution direction when necessary.

The cultural dimension also involves managing the interface between the program and the external environment. The Program Manager must manage stakeholder expectations, explore new opportunities while utilizing existing resources, and build program resilience in the face of challenges. The Program Manager must establish a collaborative cultural network among program members and teams with different goals, commitments, and professional backgrounds.

Digital Transformation Program: Change Management and IT-Enabled Program Management

Introduction to Change Management

Change Management is a comprehensive, cyclical, and structured approach used to transition an organization from its current state to a future state that delivers the expected business benefits. It helps organizations integrate and coordinate people, processes, structures, culture, and strategy. Successful organizations do not evolve randomly but rather through purposeful and dynamic strategies that foresee, influence, and effectively respond to emerging and changing external trends and events.

Change Management involves planning and structured approaches to align the organization with change. At its simplest and most effective form, change management involves working with organizational stakeholders to help them understand what the change means for them, navigate the transition to ongoing operations, and overcome any challenges. From a management perspective, this involves adjusting organizational behaviors to adapt to and sustain the change. The change management life cycle framework can help structure these processes. PMI identified the life cycle framework in the following list. Change management is not a linear process but an iterative framework that can adapt to continuously evolving situations.

i. Formulate the change: Develop a change plan by identifying the need for change, assessing readiness for change, and defining the scope of the change.

ii. Plan the change: By defining change methods, planning stakeholder engagement, and planning the transition and integration.

iii. Implement the change: Prepare for the change, mobilize stakeholders, and deliver project outputs.

iv. Manage the change transition: Transition outputs to business operations, measure adoption rates and change outcomes and benefits, and adjust plans to address any gaps.

v. Sustain the change: Sustain the change through effective communication, consultation with stakeholder representatives, perception activities, and measuring the realization of benefits.

The Relationship Between Change Management and Program Management

The program life cycle is structured in accordance with the change management life cycle. Like change management, program management is a cyclical process requiring continuous evaluation to achieve organizational change objectives. Therefore, program management is well suited for managing strategic change initiatives within organizations, as it can handle ambiguous and uncertain situations. Table 6.1 shows the alignment between the program management practices discussed in this book and the phases of change management.

Table 6.1 Alignment of program management practices with change management stages

Change management	Program management
Formulate change • Identify and clarify the need for change • Assess readiness for change • Outline the scope of change	**Identify and Formulate the Program** • Form a sponsorship team, appoint a Program Manager, and establish a Program Governance Board • Create an Organizational Strategy Map • Create a Program Strategy Map and develop a Program Mandate • Develop a Program Brief • Develop a Program Preparation Plan • Form the Program Management Team • Review and approve
Plan change • Define change methods • Plan stakeholder engagement • Plan transition and integration	**Define and Plan the Program** Develop a Program Business Case, including • Draft a Program Blueprint • Create a Benefit Profile • Develop a Benefit Map • Develop a Benefit Dependency Map • Design a Project Dossier • Design the program organizational structure • Establish Program Governance Arrangements • Review and approve
Implement change • Prepare the organization for change • Mobilize stakeholders • Deliver the program outputs	**Execute and Deliver the Program** Program benefit realization management, including • Benefit measurement
Manage change transition • Transition program outputs to business operations • Measure adoption rates and outcomes/benefits • Adjust plans to address gaps	• Benefit tracking and monitoring • Benefit delivery • Stakeholder management
Sustain change • Maintain ongoing communication and consultation with stakeholders • Conducting meaning-making activities • Measure benefit realization	**Close the Program** • Close the program • Review, update, and archive program documentation • Knowledge and experience transfer • Disband the program

The Role of IT-Enabled Program Management in the Digital Transformation

Projects are concrete means to achieve organizational strategies and objectives. Each project aims to fulfill part of the organization's mission, so the successful execution of a project can directly promote the realization of the organization's mission. Conversely, a clear mission can provide projects with clear direction and guidance. Program management is not just about completing tasks; it is an important process for realizing the organization's mission and objectives (as shown in Figure 6.2).

The mission of the news media industry is to provide accurate and impartial news reporting, promoting societal knowledge enhancement and civic engagement. To achieve this mission, the news organization would integrate and coordinate multiple projects through program management, ensuring that they collectively drive the achievement of the organizational mission. For example, simultaneously developing a digital news platform, conducting in-depth investigative reporting, and expanding social media presence.

Through effective program management, these projects can work in synergy, resources can be allocated efficiently, and redundancy and waste can be minimized. This activity ensures that each project can fully play its role, complement each other, and promote achieving overall goals. For instance, the digital news platform can provide a publishing platform for in-depth investigative reports, while the social media expansion can amplify the impact of these reports. Additionally, the program's outcomes

Implementing Organizational Strategy Through Program Management

Figure 6.2 Organizational strategy drives projects

would feed back into realizing the organization's mission, further refining and adjusting the news organization's strategies and goals. The news organization can more effectively manage multiple projects through program management, ensuring each step moves in the established direction and achieves its mission and objectives.

To successfully implement enterprise digital transformation program management, this book proposes corresponding management tools based on the IT-enabled program management life cycle, explaining how program management can bridge enterprise strategy and operations, ensuring the smooth implementation of digital strategies. The following summarizes the main tools for IT-enabled program management proposed in this book:

- **Strategy Map**: Graphically presents the organization's strategic objectives, providing direction for defining and planning the IT-enabled program. It showcases the organization's long-term vision and mission, ensuring that the program's objectives align with the organization's overall strategy.
- **Program Mandate**: Defines the vision, goals, and scope of the program, providing direction for the Program Manager. Its core focus is clarifying the program's strategic positioning and identifying key stakeholders, resource needs, and significant risks.
- **Program Blueprint**: Outlines the vision and future state of the program, providing implementation direction. It describes the program's final deliverables and business transformation blueprint in detail, defining the gap between the current state and the target state.
- **Benefit Map**: Illustrates how the program's benefits are aligned with the organization's strategic objectives, ensuring the realization of expected value. This map clearly defines the program's contribution to organizational strategy, identifying various benefits brought by the program to ensure they align with strategic objectives. Additionally, it illustrates the interrelationship between various benefits, ensuring that overall benefits support one another and ultimately achieve strategic goals. Performance indicators are set for each benefit to measure the degree of realization.

- **Benefit Dependency Map:** Details the relationship between projects within the program and their associated benefits, enabling Program Managers to identify and manage interdependencies between projects. This map clarifies the strategic objectives the program aims to achieve, lists the benefits expected from the program, and links them to strategic objectives. It identifies all projects within the program and shows each project's contribution to benefits. It presents the interdependencies between projects, benefits, and strategic objectives, ensuring project collaboration to realize overall benefits.
- **Project Dossier:** Provides detailed information for each project to enable effective management by the Program Manager, including each project's scope, objectives, deliverables, timelines, resources, and risks, ensuring that project objectives align with the overall program objectives.

Lastly, digital transformation involves multiple aspects of enterprise processes, business models, and organizational and cultural layers. IT-enabled program management is a crucial tool for realizing this transformation. It decomposes the organization's digital strategic objectives into interdependent projects and ensures the final realization of strategic goals through effective management. Traditional views suggest that an organization's strategy is crucial for setting project objectives, selecting and prioritizing projects, setting direction for projects, and ensuring that implemented projects align with the strategy. This perspective relates to research on organizational change, new product and service development, and project portfolio management, but it is not the only way to link projects with strategy. Research and practice in program management reveal the role of programs as sources of creativity. In future strategic practices, IT-enabled programs will drive organizational strategic changes (as shown in Figure 6.3).

We further illustrate the traditional enterprise digital transformation process using the Strategic Alignment Model of Henderson and Venkatraman, shown in Figure 6.4. In response to the needs of digital transformation, enterprises must review both the IT and business domains, each of which encompasses strategy, infrastructure, and processes.

Driving Organizational Strategy Renewal Through IT-Enabled
Program Management

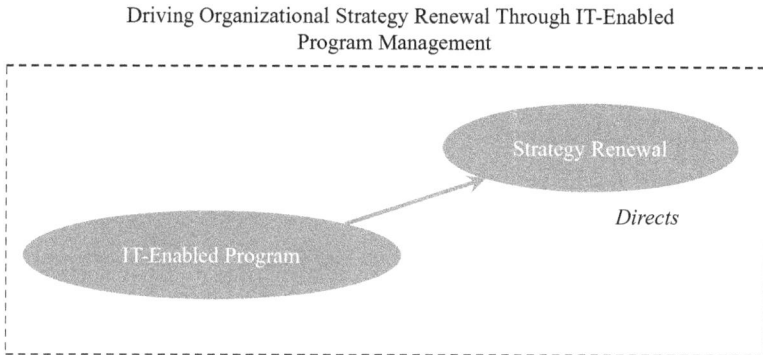

Figure 6.3 IT program driving organizational strategic change

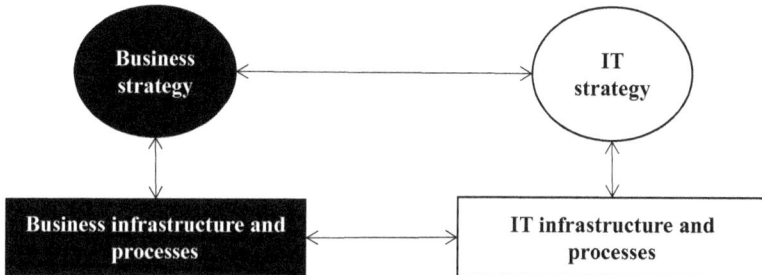

Figure 6.4 Digital transformation strategy implementation model

From a dual-variable perspective, it is necessary to pursue two types of vertical alignment and two types of horizontal alignment. Vertical alignment involves the continuous support of IT architecture and processes for IT strategy and the continuous support of organizational infrastructure and processes for business strategy. Horizontal alignment includes aligning IT and business strategies to respond to external markets and environments and connecting organizational infrastructure and processes with technological architecture and processes to address internal conflicts.

Based on the above concepts, there are four cross-stage alignment modes in digital transformation: business strategy, business infrastructure and processes, IT strategy, and IT infrastructure and processes. These four modes include:

- **System Integration Phase**: For example, enterprise system unification, where ERP (Enterprise Resource Planning) systems are integrated to centralize and automate financial, human resources, and supply chain management, thus improving data consistency and accuracy and enhancing operational efficiency.

- **Technology Transformation Phase**: For instance, big data technology can collect and analyze customer shopping behaviors and preferences, enabling more precise marketing, improving customer satisfaction, and increasing sales.
- **Technology Competitive Potential Phase**: Reengineering business processes through extensive customer information to achieve more flexible delivery services.
- **Technology Service Phase**: For instance, creating new digital services or digital business models based on the new technological capabilities and business processes established in the previous phases.

The first two phases are driven by business strategy, while the latter two are driven by IT strategy. Enterprises will dynamically repeat these four alignment phases in digital transformation until they fully integrate their new business and IT strategies, ultimately completing the digital transformation and forming a new digital business strategy.

Notably, after organizations establish new IT capabilities and infrastructure in the first two phases, the IT strategy will trigger changes in business strategy in the third and fourth phases. IT-enabled programs drive strategic changes and execute each of these four alignment phases.

Therefore, in the digital age, IT-enabled programs will provide a comprehensive update of organizational strategy. This update encompasses not only technological improvements but also innovations in business models, operational efficiency enhancements, customer experience optimizations, and substantial market competitiveness increases. The successful implementation of IT-enabled programs will enable enterprises to maintain agility and adaptability in a rapidly changing digital environment, ultimately achieving sustained business growth and long-term strategic objectives.

Encouragement and Expectations

One should have the following expectations for IT-enabled program management.

Goal-Driven Strategy Implementation

This book argues the importance of benefit realization and measurement. In practice, the tools provided in this book, such as the Strategy Map, Benefit Map, and Benefit Dependency Map, can be used to plan goal-driven IT-enabled organizational transformation strategies with reverse engineering thinking, helping enterprises enhance overall control and insight into programs, and achieve precise implementation of strategic goals.

Enterprise Development

Program management models help enterprises save costs, create benefits, and address challenges such as professional personnel shortages and team allocation difficulties. Therefore, in practice, the concepts mentioned in this book, as well as the program management tools provided, can be used as a training foundation to establish a cultivation mechanism for Program Managers, enhancing their strategic insight, leadership, and professional skills in complex environments, and ensuring they can flexibly respond to rapidly changing needs.

Organizational Culture and Change Management

The success of digital transformation depends on cultural change within the organization. In the future, change management should be further strengthened to ensure that organizational culture can adapt to the collaboration needs and strategic orientation of programs, promoting smooth implementation of strategies.

Personnel Integration and Talent Development

Program management facilitates personnel integration, optimizes personnel allocation, and refines management responsibilities, enabling employees to unlock their full potential. During implementation, employees continuously engage with new fields, learn new knowledge, and master new technologies, providing training pathways for developing versatile talents within the enterprise.

Resource Sharing and Benefit Maximization

The program management model enables resource sharing among related projects within the enterprise, ensuring the full utilization of resources and the smooth implementation of each project. Through systematic and mature management thinking, seamless communication is achieved between subprojects under the program management team, ensuring the timely allocation of human and material resources and the sharing of successful experiences.

Establish Repeatable Processes

Realize that transformation is never linear. It doesn't end when a program concludes. Instead, it evolves with the market, internal dynamics, and institutional forces. Strategies are continually revisited, programs reshaped, and failed paths abandoned. A successful transformation doesn't rely on a single program, but on robust, adaptive program governance mechanisms capable of continuous iteration.

Conclusion

Digital transformation, by its nature, is not a one-time project—it is an ongoing, evolving journey. Once begun, it does not truly come to an end. New technologies, market shifts, and societal expectations will continue to reshape the digital landscape. In this context, each program should be viewed as a dynamic response to specific stages of transformation. The life cycle tools introduced in Chapters 2 through 5 provide a foundational framework for managing each of these programs. Over time, organizations will initiate new programs to respond to emerging needs, and each of those will cycle through the same fundamental phases outlined in this book.

However, program management is not a magic bullet. It does not provide a one-size-fits-all solution to the complex challenges of digital transformation. However, it offers a structured, flexible, and scalable approach that organizations can adopt to manage and execute strategic initiatives with clarity and direction. When implemented effectively, IT-enabled program management serves as a critical bridge between organizational strategy and operational execution, enabling organizations to navigate uncertainty and realize their digital ambitions.

By internalizing and applying the tools of IT-enabled program management, practitioners can gain a firmer grasp of how to orchestrate strategic change. This book aims not to provide an exhaustive solution, but rather to serve as a practical and conceptual foundation—one that inspires professionals to think systematically, lead confidently, and build programs prepared for the demands of digital transformation.

Complementary Reading

Henderson, J. C., and H. Venkatraman. 1993. "Strategic Alignment: Leveraging Information Technology for Transforming Organizations." *IBM Systems Journal* 38 (2.3): 472–484.

PMI (Project Management Institute). 2017. *The Standard for Program Management.* 4th ed. PMI.

Case Practice—Digital Transformation of Datong Textile

This case is a fictional scenario. The content of the case is written in accordance with the requirements outlined in the chapters of this book. All characters, names, titles, and other information are fictional and do not represent actual events.

Case Background

The Opportunity for Datong Textile's Transformation

A small, tin-roofed Tainan building boasts a rich textile and manufacturing history. Datong Textile, established over 40 years ago, previously achieved annual revenues exceeding 8 billion New Taiwan Dollars (NT$). However, recent performance has plummeted over the past year, with the weaving, dyeing, and garment departments experiencing declining revenues for three consecutive quarters, causing significant concern for Chairman Raymond.

After observing the success of the automated and digitally transformed factory at Hongchang Manufacturing, Raymond began to seriously consider the digital transformation advocated by the Deputy Manager of the Sales Department (Raymond's son Peter). Peter hoped a transformation could address the declining performance and align with market trends. Could digital transformation bring new possibilities to Datong Textile?

Obstacles to Digital Transformation

Datong Textile was an early adopter of ERP systems in the industry. Digital technology is not as unfamiliar to this manufacturing plant as one might think. The collaboration of old, middle-aged, and young generations of machines and workers has repeatedly produced textile miracles at Datong Textile. However, a digital transformation has several challenges and obstacles that await Raymond and Peter.

Obstacle 1: Despite years of ERP system usage and the accumulation of massive data, the system's primary application remains limited to managing materials, orders, procurement, costs, and inventory. The current value is primarily evident in the production of monthly reports, with limited additional applications.

Obstacle 2: The textile industry involves numerous complex technical processes, and Datong Textile boasts a team of outstanding and experienced masters. These experts use their refined skills and robust experience to fulfill various customized needs by comparing dye properties, temperature control, and fabric combinations. Introducing automated production equipment would require employees to abandon production processes they have been accustomed to for one or two decades, adapt to entirely new work models, and face the challenges of learning and applying these new methods. Can employees quickly master such technology? How can we teach machines what people have taken so long to learn? The General Manager of the Garment Manufacturing Department, Kevin, and a senior employee, Allen, expressed significant doubts about this challenge.

Obstacle 3: For employees, the leadership's decision to pursue digital transformation might make them feel like they are about to be replaced by machines. Automation is not seen as a tool to reduce workload but as a competitor poised to replace and lay off workers. Kevin, who will turn 65 in three years, is one of Datong's first employees. Trusted by Raymond, Kevin has previously led the Garment Manufacturing Department and is familiar with the equipment, jokingly referred to as "the Eight-Nation Alliance" within the company. He can always find a solution to any equipment problem. "I remember we spent a lot of money to introduce the ERP system," Allen said worriedly, "Some employees couldn't adapt to the conflicts during the introduction process and resigned. Now, installing sensors on the machines to collect data might make employees feel monitored, leading them to believe the company is using automation to replace them, potentially even laying them off. This will cause unrest in the company."

The Key to Digital Transformation

Datong Textile possesses extensive manufacturing experience and excellent technical personnel with a history of using digital tools. However, how can the entire organization integrate digital transformation technologies and core principles more efficiently to respond to a volatile market and keep pace with industry and client automation trends? Where should digital transformation be applied to achieve cost reduction, risk mitigation, and significant results in the current organization?

Digital Transformation of Datong Textile

Transformation Core

Chairman Raymond believes that digital transformation is no longer optional but a necessary strategy to keep the company competitive and ahead of the market. To ensure a return on investment, Peter proposed to the board that digital transformation should increase production efficiency by 50 percent, reduce material losses by 30 percent, and restore annual revenue to over NT$7.5 billion within three years. Peter's dual-core digital transformation plan encompasses smart manufacturing in the weaving and dyeing department, as well as automation in the garment manufacturing department, integrating both with the ERP system to achieve the vision of servitization in manufacturing. Peter's dual-core transformation involves technological changes and a new business model perspective. He aims to make Datong Textile a globally leading, smart textile company, enabling real-time connectivity and immediate response from raw material procurement to production to sales.

Indeed, the promotion of the two cores requires a sequence. In dyeing and finishing, collecting and integrating production data from various machines and using big data analysis to optimize production processes can make dyeing and finishing operations more efficient and cost-competitive in the short term. In the long term, accumulated data can further predict fabric and color trends, providing valuable insights to customers.

For garment manufacturing operations requiring primarily labor, Peter hopes to optimize processes through automation, saving time and labor, and enhancing market responsiveness. New business models may emerge, such as localized service centers that complete the entire process from sampling and production to shipping quickly, becoming satellite factories that overcome labor-intensive regional constraints and supply chain production and transportation challenges. These centers can stay close to the end market to develop new customers.

Raymond remembered that company shareholders are already paying attention to this matter, and without some achievements, it would be difficult to gain their support for the digital transformation. Moreover, at the plan's initial stage, employees tend to adopt a wait-and-see attitude to determine if this transformation is a significant upheaval or merely a fleeting idea from the leadership.

Emphasis on Long-Term R&D Culture

Fortunately, the concept of R&D is deeply ingrained in Datong's DNA. Annually, Datong invests[7] percent of its funds in innovation and R&D, establishing capabilities for fabric product identification. With over 160 high-end patents and the production speed of more than 1,500 types of fabrics per year, Datong competes globally.

Datong is accustomed to being on the path of change. Transforming every five years is a regular internal management goal. The wave of digitization and high-tech advancements has not overtaken this long-standing company but has leveraged it to become Taiwan's first factory to complete an Industry 4.0 deployment. This transformation has resulted in lower production costs, reduced defect rates, and improved fabric quality.

Industry Trends: Real Market and Business Environment Needs

Datong Textile's General Manager stated, "Industry 4.0 is not just about machine automation but looking at the entire production process." The key element of Industry 4.0 is mass customization. Most current orders are small batches with diverse and complex details. Implementing smart solutions can achieve small-batch production while maintaining the low cost of mass production.

Additionally, labor shortages have been a significant pain point for Taiwan's traditional manufacturing in recent years. Smart solutions address this issue, allowing existing experts to focus more time and energy on valuable gaps such as knowledge transfer.

From Traditional Factories to Smart Factories, from Manual to Data Management

Located in Taiwan, ICT (Information and Communication Technology) is a notable local advantage. Many difficulties can be resolved through technology provided by Taiwanese companies. Therefore, in addition to using Germany's SAP services for the cloud platform, Datong extensively adopts local Industry 4.0 solutions, connecting with 110 local ICT manufacturers and enabling real-time, networked operations. Sensors on the machines collect data during production, which is initially organized in the ERP system and then uploaded to the cloud for data analysis.

Datong began studying its needs for Industry 4.0 10 years prior and quickly decided to invest NT$450 million in a three-year smart factory transformation plan. Datong invested NT$100 million in the first year to achieve production line intelligence, with a return on investment within the first year.

The dyeing and finishing plant saw the fastest progress in smart transformation. All production equipment is networked, achieving machine-to-machine communication and real-time status monitoring in Industry 4.0. The factory no longer has a large number of operators moving back and forth. This process optimization reduces time-consuming and error-prone manual data monitoring, as well as the risk of machine failure or personnel misallocation. This optimization has yielded remarkable results for Datong: Dyeing 500 yards of fabric previously took three hours; now, it takes only a third of that time. Material loss decreased by 6 percent, and fabric dyeing accuracy increased by 5 percent, translating to an annual benefit of NT$95 million.

Through the smart factory upgrade of Industry 4.0, Datong can more accurately manage materials, improve dyeing accuracy, and reduce production time for small-batch and customized production needs. Along with its strong R&D capabilities, Datong's advantages are highlighted when competing for orders from global competitors. This upgrade represents the value that Industry 4.0 brings to traditional factories, enhancing productivity and competitiveness.

Discussion Preface

The program management tools introduced in this book apply to digital transformation programs. However, when discussing the case "Digital Transformation of Datong Textile," it is essential to consider the contextual differences between this case and the example case "Digital Transformation of *The Sun News*" in this book. It is necessary to evaluate the differences in the analysis process and content when applying the book's analysis techniques. The following explanation provides a reference for discussing this case study.

Category	*The Sun News*	Datong Textile
Transformation Background and Opportunity	Adjust business model to adapt to the digital age, enhancing digital presentation and interaction of news.	Enhance production efficiency and lower costs through digitization, enabling rapid response to market demands.
Main Challenges and Obstacles	Transforming news production processes, enhancing journalists' digital skills while maintaining news quality, and increasing traffic and reader interaction.	Facing technological adaptation challenges, integrating new automated equipment and digital tools, and addressing employee concerns about job security due to the transformation.
Process Differences	Focus on digital innovation in content and reader interaction.	Emphasize automation and efficiency improvement in production processes.
Technology Application	Primarily involves information technology and new media tools	Focus on investment in manufacturing technology and industrial automation.
Personnel Training	Emphasize digital media skills and innovative content creation.	Focus on skills enhancement for operating new equipment and technologies.
Stakeholder Analysis	Stakeholder analysis focuses on internal department heads, employees, and the external audience.	Stakeholder analysis focuses on internal department heads, employees, and external supply chain vendors and customers.

Discussion Items

Descriptive, text-only solutions follow the list of discussion questions. Try formulating answers first, or consider those provided below, and then devise an alternative plan. There is usually more than one possible strategy for an organization's digital transformation. Use the information to generate accompanying visual documents.

1. What is Datong Textile's new organizational strategy? Why do they need a program? What is the vision of the program? (Chapter 2)
2. Draw Datong Textile's Organizational Strategy Map. (Chapter 2)
3. Create Datong Textile's Program Mandate and Program Brief. (Chapter 2)

4. Create Datong Textile's Program Blueprint. (Chapter 3)
5. Draw Datong Textile's Program Benefit Map. (Chapter 3)
6. Referencing Table 4.1, organize the program benefit measurement indicators and performance indicators. (Chapter 4)

Reference Information for the Datong Textile Practice Case

1. What is Datong Textile's new organizational strategy? Why do they need a program? What is the vision of the program? (Chapter 2)

   New Organizational Strategy: Datong Textile's new organizational strategy centers on digital transformation, aiming to enhance production efficiency and lower costs while responding promptly to market demands. This strategy involves implementing smart manufacturing in the weaving and dyeing department, as well as automating the garment manufacturing department, and integrating their processes with the ERP system to achieve servitization in manufacturing.

   Need for a Program: Datong Textile needs a program to:
   - *Coordinate and manage multiple interrelated projects.*
   - *Ensure alignment with the overall strategic objectives.*
   - *Optimize resource allocation and avoid redundancy.*
   - *Monitor and measure progress and outcomes effectively.*
   - *Facilitate the adoption of new technologies and processes.*

   Vision of the Program: The program's vision is to transform Datong Textile into a globally leading smart textile company that can connect and respond in real-time across the entire value chain—from raw material procurement to production and sales. The program aims to achieve significant efficiency gains, cost reductions, and enhanced market responsiveness.

2. Draw Datong Textile's Organizational Strategy Map based on the first question. (Chapter 2)

   Datong Textile's Organizational Strategy Map:
   - *Vision: To become a globally leading smart textile company.*
   - *Strategic Objectives:*
     - *Improve Production Efficiency: Increase production efficiency by 50 percent within three years.*

- *Reduce Material Loss: Decrease material loss by 30 percent.*
- *Revenue Growth: Restore annual revenue to over NT$7.5 billion.*
- *Enhance Market Responsiveness: Implement flexible production capabilities to meet market demands swiftly.*
  - *Key Initiatives:*
    - *Smart Manufacturing: Implement smart manufacturing in the weaving and dyeing department.*
    - *Automation: Automate the garment manufacturing department.*
    - *Integration with ERP: Integrate smart manufacturing and automation with the ERP system to streamline operations.*
  - *Supportive Actions:*
    - *Employee Training: Enhance skills for operating new equipment and technologies.*
    - *Technology Investment: Invest in manufacturing technology and industrial automation.*
    - *Stakeholder Engagement: Involve internal departments, employees, supply chain vendors, and customers in the transformation process to ensure a comprehensive approach.*
  - *Expected Outcomes:*
    - *Operational Excellence: Achieve lower production costs, reduced defects, and improved fabric quality.*
    - *Customer Satisfaction: Improve customer satisfaction and expand the customer base.*
    - *Competitive Advantage: Enhance competitiveness in the global market.*

3. Please create Datong Textile's Program Mandate and Program Brief. (Chapter 2)

   Program Mandate:
   - *Vision: Transform Datong Textile into a globally leading smart textile company.*
   - *Goals:*
     - *Increase production efficiency by 50 percent within three years.*
     - *Reduce material loss by 30 percent.*
     - *Restore annual revenue to over NT$7.5 billion.*

- ○ **Scope:** *Implement smart manufacturing in the weaving and dyeing department, automate the garment manufacturing department, and integrate these with the ERP system.*
- ○ **Key Stakeholders:** *Chairman, board members, senior management, department heads, employees, supply chain vendors, and customers*
- ○ **Resources Required:** *Investment in new technologies, employee training programs, and consulting services for digital transformation*
- ○ **Major Risks:** *Resistance to change from employees, technological integration challenges, and potential disruptions during the transition*

Program Brief:

- ○ **Feasibility Assessment:** *Evaluate the technical feasibility of implementing smart manufacturing and automation, as well as the financial viability of the proposed investments.*
- ○ **Objectives:**
  - *Achieve significant efficiency gains and cost reductions.*
  - *Enhance market responsiveness and customer satisfaction.*
- ○ **Expected Benefits:**
  - *Improved operational efficiency and reduced production costs*
  - *Enhanced fabric quality and reduced defects*
  - *Increased customer satisfaction and market competitiveness*
- ○ **Potential Risks:**
  - *Employee resistance to new technologies*
  - *Integration challenges with existing systems*
  - *Initial disruptions during the implementation phase*
- ○ Timeline: *Three-year plan with phased implementation*
4. Please create Datong Textile's Program Blueprint. (Chapter 3)

Program Blueprint:

- ○ **Vision:** *Datong Textile will become a globally leading smart textile company characterized by real-time connectivity and responsiveness across its entire value chain.*
- ○ **Future State:**
  - **Weaving and Dyeing Department:** *Smart manufacturing implemented with real-time data collection and analysis, optimized production processes, and predictive capabilities for fabric and color trends.*

- ***Garment Manufacturing Department:*** *Automated production processes with reduced labor requirements, faster production cycles, and the ability to provide rapid, localized services.*
- ***ERP Integration:*** *Seamless integration of smart manufacturing and automation with the ERP system, enabling centralized data management and real-time decision making.*
  - ○ ***Current State Versus Future State:***
    - ***Current State:*** *Manual production processes, limited use of digital tools, and significant labor requirements*
    - ***Future State:*** *Automated and optimized production processes, extensive use of digital tools, and reduced labor requirements*
  - ○ ***Implementation Phases:***
    - ***Phase 1:*** *Implement smart manufacturing in the weaving and dyeing department.*
    - ***Phase 2:*** *Automate the garment manufacturing department.*
    - ***Phase 3:*** *Integrate smart manufacturing and automation with the ERP system.*

5. Draw Datong Textile's Program Benefit Map. (Chapter 3)

   Datong Textile's Program Benefit Map:
   - ○ ***Strategic Objective:*** *Improve Production Efficiency*
     - ***Benefit:*** *50 percent increase in production efficiency*
     - ***Project:*** *Implement smart manufacturing in the weaving and dyeing department*
     - ***Indicator:*** *Production efficiency metrics*
   - ○ ***Strategic Objective:*** *Reduce Material Loss*
     - ***Benefit:*** *30 percent reduction in material loss*
     - ***Project:*** *Automate the garment manufacturing department*
     - ***Indicator:*** *Material loss metrics*
   - ○ ***Strategic Objective:*** *Revenue Growth*
     - ***Benefit:*** *Restore annual revenue to over NT$7.5 billion*
     - ***Project:*** *Integrate smart manufacturing and automation with the ERP system*
     - ***Indicator:*** *Revenue metrics*
   - ○ ***Strategic Objective:*** *Enhance Market Responsiveness*
     - ***Benefit:*** *Improved market responsiveness and customer satisfaction*

- **Project:** *Implement flexible production capabilities and localized services*
- **Indicator:** *Customer satisfaction metrics and market response times*

6. Referencing Table 4.1, organize the program benefit measurement indicators and performance indicators. (Chapter 4)

Benefit	Measurement indicator	Performance indicator
50% increase in production efficiency	Production efficiency metrics	Percentage increase in production efficiency
30% reduction in material loss	Material loss metrics	Percentage reduction in material loss
Restore annual revenue to over NT$7.5 billion	Revenue metrics	Annual revenue figures
Improved market responsiveness and customer satisfaction	Customer satisfaction metrics, market response times	Customer satisfaction scores, average market response times

Complementary Reading

Anthony, S. D., C. G. Gilbert, and M. W. Johnson. 2017. *Dual Transformation: How to Reposition Today's Business While Creating the Future*. Harvard Business Review Press.

Flint, Y. 2025. *Innovative Business Development: Implementing Transformation from Within*. Business Expert Press.

Jiang, J., G. Klein, and W. Huang. 2020. *Projects, Programs, and Portfolios in Strategic Organizational Transformation*. Business Expert Press.

Lee, R. T. 2018. *Strategic Cost Transformation: Using Business Domain Management to Improve Cost Data, Analysis, and Management*. Business Expert Press.

Leinwand, P., and M. M. Mani. 2022. *Beyond Digital: How Great Leaders Transform Their Organizations and Shape the Future*. Harvard Business Press.

Mattingly, L. C. 2018. *Managing Organizational Change: The Measurable Benefits of Applied IOCM*. Business Expert Press.

McKeown, N., and M. Durkin. 2017. *The Seven Principles of Digital Business Strategy*. Business Expert Press.

Pachory, A. 2019. *Aligning Technology with Business for Digital Transformation: Plugging in IT to Light up Your Business*. Business Expert Press.

Paquette, P., and M. Frankl. 2015. *Agile Project Management for Business Transformation Success*. Business Expert Press.

Piney, C. 2017. *Earned Benefit Management: Aligning, Realizing, and Sustaining Strategy*. Auerbach Publications.

PMI (Project Management Institute). 2017. *The Standard for Program Management*. 4th ed. PMI.

PMI (Project Management Institute). 2024. *Risk Management in Portfolios, Programs, and Projects: A Practice Guide*. PMI.

Prabhu, A. 2025. *Digital Leadership Framework: Cultivating the Four Key Competencies*. Business Expert Press.

Serra, C. E. M. 2016. *Benefits Realization Management: Strategic Value from Portfolios, Programs, and Projects*. Auerbach Publications.

The Stationery Office. 2011. *Managing Successful Programmes (MSP)*. 4th ed. AXELOS.

Waddock, S. 2023. *Catalyzing Transformation: Making System Change Happen*. Business Expert Press.

Washington, M. 2011. *Successful Organizational Transformation: The Five Critical Elements*. Business Expert Press.

Westerman, G., D. Bonnet, and A. McAfee. 2014. *Leading Digital: Turning Technology into Business Transformation*. Harvard Business Press.

Glossary

Ambiguity: The causal relationships are entirely unclear, with no established precedents, and involve unknown variables.

Benefit Dependency Map: A tool for planning benefits that presents the benefits and the related activities needed to achieve these benefits. It helps to identify and understand the changes or strategic actions required to realize a specific benefit.

Benefit Map: A tool for identifying benefits developed progressively from the Program Blueprint.

Benefit Profile: A tool for defining benefits, providing measurable indicators for each benefit, and serving as a planning and control tool to track the progress of subsequent deliveries and benefit realization.

Benefits Ranking: The process of prioritizing the benefits provided by a program based on their relative importance, impact, or strategic alignment.

Benefit Realization Management: Framework for managing the life cycle phases of benefit realization, including identification, execution, and maintenance phases.

Benefits Valuing: The process of quantifying each benefit using financial or non-financial metrics to assess its value.

Benefit: Improvements or enhancements that the program delivers, contributing to the achievement of the organization's strategic goals.

Business Change Manager: Responsible individual for achieving benefits by transitioning capabilities into business operations and facilitating business changes to leverage new capabilities, complementing the role of the Program Manager.

Business Change: Changes occurring in the business or operational environment, typically involving new ways of working or new business states.

Business Project: Projects based on organizational development and processes.

Capability: Implemented project outputs as operational outcomes.

Change Management: A comprehensive, cyclical, and structured approach to transitioning an organization from its current state to a future state with anticipated business benefits.

Change of Boundary: Changes in the defined scope of a project due to external driving factors, such as market environment changes.

Change Program: Coordinating multiple interdependent change projects to achieve integrated benefits from aggregating multiple projects.

Change Project: Projects that are adjusted in response to external changes to fit a highly uncertain and ambiguous current state.

Clan Control: Control exerted through shared values or behavioral norms related to organizational culture, enhancing members' organizational awareness and value alignment.

Complexity: Involves many interconnected parts and variables, with some information available or predictable; however, the volume or nature of the information makes it difficult to manage effectively.

Digital Leadership: Beyond traditional leadership skills, it emphasizes digital literacy, requiring a deep understanding of the significance and value of digital transformation, as well as the ability to break down digital transformation strategies.

Digital Optimization: Further familiarizing and optimizing digital tools to improve operational efficiency and enhance customer satisfaction after digitization.

Digital Transformation: Comprehensive organizational change primarily by introducing digital technologies and artificial intelligence to alter business operations, processes, and models to meet evolving market and customer demands.

Digitalization: Reducing operational costs by introducing digital tools like cloud management and the Internet-of-Things.

Enabler: Something that can be developed, built, or acquired, usually from outside the organization.

Execute the Benefit: Through project execution, new capabilities from project outputs are established, and these capabilities are applied in daily operations to generate outcomes in an iterative and recursive process.

Formulate the Change: Develop a change plan by identifying change needs, assessing readiness, and defining the scope of the change.

Identify the Benefit: The leadership identifies the benefits expected from achieving the program's goals.

Identifying Pre-Program: Early-stage activities of the program, including initiating organizational transformation strategies, establishing a sponsorship group, forming the program management team, and planning pre-program activities.

Implement the Change: Preparing for change, mobilizing stakeholders, and delivering project outputs to facilitate the implementation of the change.

Integrated Benefit: Effectively aggregating various benefits provided by the program.

IT-Enabled Program Management: Incorporating IT into multiple related IT projects and auxiliary projects within the organization, providing IT-based value to meet stakeholder needs.

IT-Enabled Program: A program implementing digitalization strategies.

IT Project: Projects based on IT infrastructure and processes.

IT-Based Value: The results of IT-enabled program management.

Iterative Process: An iterative process involves repeatedly refining and advancing the next phase based on feedback, with previous iterations serving as the basis for subsequent ones, achieving the final required goals or outcomes. Specifically, it refers to adjustments between different stages of the program life cycle.

Manage the Change Transition: Transition outputs into business operations, measure adoption rates and change results, and adjust plans to address gaps and manage the change transition.

Organization Strategy Map: A tool for visualizing and concretizing organizational strategy.

Organizational Transformational Change Strategy: New organizational strategies designed in response to external environmental changes to achieve transformation goals.

Outcome: The results of applying new capabilities to organizational changes, typically affecting organizational behavior or conditions.

Plan the Change: Planning change by defining change methods, planning stakeholder engagement, and managing transitions and integration.

Program Benefit Identifying, Defining, and Planning: Identifying the benefits to be achieved, defining the indicators and performance metrics for the benefits, and planning the required project outputs, capabilities, and outcomes for the program.

Program Blueprint: Describes the current state, anticipated future state, and the gap between the current and future states.

Program Brief: Expands on the Program Mandate to define specific goals, expected benefits, potential risks, cost estimates, and timelines to confirm achievable benefits and conduct feasibility assessments.

Program Business Case: Summarizes the scope, direction, goals, costs, benefits, schedule, and risks related to the program to evaluate its feasibility.

Program Governance Arrangement: Describes the program's governance approach.

Program Governance Board: Composed of individuals with management responsibilities and decision-making authority to ensure that the program is managed according to plan and to review, advise, and track progress to deliver planned outcomes and benefits.

Program Management Maps: Tools to help Program Managers identify, define, and plan the benefits the program should achieve.

Program Management Office: The central hub and information center for the program, responsible for coordinating information, communication, monitoring, and control activities.

Program Manager: Responsible for leading and managing the program, communicating with the governance board, delivering new capabilities, and achieving benefits until the end of the program.

Program Mandate: Describes the results required from the program based on the organization's strategic goals, outlining the vision, scope, budget, and timeline.

Program Organizational Structure: Describes the composition of the program's organization to ensure it meets governance and management needs in the changing context.

Program Preparation Plan: Plans the governance, resources, and expected timelines of the program, identifies participants, considers resource delivery, and outlines the program's application assurance.

Program Sponsor: The individual who initially recognizes the need for organizational change and initiates the program.

Program Strategy Map: Visually describes the organization's strategic goals and their relationships with the program.

Program Vision Statement: Describes the future state after the program's delivery to attract more stakeholders and secure their support and commitment.

Project Dossier: Details the information about the projects and activities forming the program and describes how executing these projects will deliver capabilities to the organization and the expected results and benefits.

Project Output: The projects required to establish new capabilities.

Senior Responsible Owner: The formal title of the individual with the highest management authority in the program.

Sponsoring Group: A group formed by the Program Sponsor, consisting of members with strategic interests in the program and decision-making authority over organizational investments and capital expenditures, thereby influencing the change's advancement.

Stakeholder Map: A visual tool showing key stakeholders in various change activities.

Stakeholder Profile: Records stakeholders' roles, names, habits, interest in change activities within the program, their impact on the outcomes, and their specific interests in the program.

Supporting Project: Secondary projects that assist in advancing the main projects.

Sustain the Benefit: Achieving and continuously providing the advantages or benefits realized from the program is the final activity in benefit delivery.

Sustain the Change: Continue the change through effective communication, consultation, and stakeholder representation, while also measuring the realization of benefits.

Uncertainty: Basic causal relationships are known despite lacking information, with possible but unpredictable changes.

Volatility: Unexpected or unstable, with unknown duration but not necessarily difficult to understand; relevant solutions are usually available.

VUCA: An acronym for four characteristics of transformational strategic goals: Volatility, Uncertainty, Complexity, and Ambiguity.

About the Authors

James J. Jiang is Distinguished Professor of Information Management, College of Management, National Taiwan University (NTU), Taiwan. Before joining NTU, he was Distinguished Professor of Information Systems (IS) at the Australian National University in Canberra, Australia, and Professor of Information Systems at the University of Central Florida, the United States. Prof. Jiang has taught project and program management courses at every level, including undergraduate, MBA, Professional MBA, and Executive MBA students, in programs rated among the best internationally. He directed some of the earliest doctoral dissertations on program management, including interteam dependencies, attainment of strategic goals, cross-functional programs, and IT-enabled program governance topics. Prof. Jiang's research interests remain focused on IT project management and IT program management within the IS/IT discipline. He has published over 200 journal articles in these areas and has been ranked among the most productive IS researchers globally. Prof. Jiang served as Senior Editor for *MIS Quarterly* and the *Journal of the Association for Information Systems*. He is the Editor-in-Chief of the *Pacific Asia Journal of the Association for Information Systems* and a Fellow of the Association for Information Management (AIS).

Gary Klein retired as the Couger Professor of Information Systems from the University of Colorado, Colorado Springs. Before pursuing an academic career, Gary consulted as part of an international consulting group and was director of the information systems department for a major financial institution. He served as Director of Education for IPMA-USA (International Project Management Association, United States) and retains an active membership. His areas of expertise include project and program management, information system development, and technology transfer, with over 250 publications in these areas. He is a Fellow of the Decision Sciences Institute, where he advanced the Specific Interest Group in Project Management. Gary held prior editorial posts with *MIS Quarterly*, the *Journal of the Association for Information Systems*, *Comparative Technology Transfer and Society*, the *International Journal of Information Technology Project Management*, the *Pacific Asia Journal of the Association for Information Systems*, *Organizational Cybersecurity Journal*, and as co-Editor-in-Chief for the Project Management Institute's *Project Management Journal*.

Judy Y. H. Huang is a PhD candidate at the Graduate Institute of Business Administration at National Taiwan University, Taiwan (NTU). She obtained her BS and MS degrees in Information Systems (IS) and is currently pursuing her PhD on scholarship. Her research interests are in IT program management and IT program governance. She has published journal articles on project management and IS. Her doctoral dissertation focuses on IT-enabled program governance, exploring how the IT program board makes effective decisions. Additionally, she serves as an instructional assistant for courses on IT project management and transformation program management at NTU. She is a member of the Project Management Institute and the Association for Information Systems.

Index

Agile adaptation management, 18–19
Alignment responsibility
  downward, 16–17
  upward, 15–16
Ambidextrous management, 19–20
Ambiguity, 18, 115, 116, 126–127

Benefit Dependency Map, 73, 79, 85,
  119, 125, 138, 146
Benefit Map, 105, 106, 145
  completed, 107
  identifying benefits, 80–82
  Program Management Maps, 79–80
  to report benefit realization
    progress, 110–112
  revised program, 107
Benefit Profile, 73, 79, 108, 112, 115
  purpose, 82
  The Sun News, 83
Benefit realization
  Benefit Map to report, 110
  benefit realization plan, 103
  delivering and measuring, 105–109
  identifying benefits, 102
  managing, 102–105
  monitoring, 112–115
  The Sun News, 110, 112
  sustain benefits, 103–105
  tracking, 109–110
Benefit realization management
  (BRM), 101, 102
Benefits achievement, 111, 113–114
Benefits management, 92
Benefits measurement indicators, 108
Brand awareness, 109
Brand reputation, 109
Business Change Manager
  (BCM), 95–96
Business Changes, 80
Business model transformation, 2
Business process transformation, 2
Business projects, 11

Capabilities, 80, 85
Change Management, 141–142
  organizational culture and, 149
  and Program Management,
    142–143
Change program, 4
Change project, 4
Clan control, 11
Closing IT-enabled program phase,
  11–12, 129–130, 139
  disbanding, 132
  documentation, 131–132
  key points, 130
  lessons learned feedback,
    132–133
  reviewing, 131
  risk considerations, 133–134
  signs to close early, 131
Cloud management, 1
Complexity, 18, 115, 116, 126–127
Conflict management, integrated, 19
Connection responsibility,
  interfacing, 17–18
Core program management task, 13
Cultural transformation, 2
Customer benefits, 105

Datong Textile case, 151–162
Defining and planning IT-enabled
  program phase, 10–11,
  138–139
  checklist, 98
  developing Program Business
    Case, 71–96
  review and approval of Program
    Business Case, 96–97
  risk considerations, 97–98
Delivering benefits, 105–109
Digital equipment and
  technology, 85
Digital leadership, 21
Digital literacy, 21

Digital Optimization, 1
Digital strategy, 24
    and digital operations, 3–4, 7
    execution, 6
    soft landing for, 5–7
Digital transformation, 1–3, 137.
        See also IT-enabled
        management program
    Datong Textile case, 151–162
    digital strategy and digital
        operations, 3–4
    program management, 3–7
    soft landing for digital strategy, 5–7
    The Sun News case. See The
        Sun News
Digitalization, 1
Downward alignment responsibility,
        16–17
Dynamic stakeholder coordination,
        20–21

Enablers, 80
Execute the benefit realization
        plan, 103
Executing and delivering IT-enabled
        program phase, 11, 139
    checklist, 127
    monitoring program delivery,
        101–115
    risk considerations, 126–127
    stakeholder communication
        management, 115–125

Financial benefits, 104
Formulate the change, 142
Formulating program
    Program Brief, 58–62
    Program Mandate, 52–57
    Program Preparation Plan, 62–66
    Program Strategy Map, 50–52

Goal-driven strategy
        implementation, 149
Governance, 92
    elements of program, 92–94
    paradoxes of program, 19–20
    roles within program
        organization, 88

Identify the benefits, 73, 74, 77
Identifying and formulating
        IT-enabled program phase,
        8, 10, 35, 138
    approval to proceed, 66–67
    checklist, 68
    formulating program. See
        Formulating program
    identifying pre-program. See
        Identifying pre-program
    risk considerations, 67–68
Identifying pre-program, 35–50
    Organizational Transformation
        Strategy, initiating, 35–36
    planning pre-program. See
        Planning pre-program
    Program Management Team, 38–40
    Sponsoring Group, 36–38
Implement the change, 142
Information management strategy,
        92, 94
Integrated benefit, 4
Integrated conflict management, 19
Interfacing connection responsibility,
        17–18
Internet-of-Things, 1
IT-based value, 7, 11
IT-enabled management program,
        7–8, 137, 144–148
    alignment with business strategy, 12
    benefit realization capabilities,
        13–14
    benefits and risk management, 13
    closing, 11–12, 139
    cognition for learning, 21–24
    competencies for managers, 18–21
    core functions of managers, 14–24
    cultural dimension, 141
    defining and planning, 10–11,
        138–139
    enterprise development, 149
    executing and delivering, 11, 139
    goal-driven strategy
        implementation, 149
    identifying and formulating,
        8, 10, 138
    learning from experience and the
        environment, 14

life cycle, 8–12
organizational culture and change
    management, 149
personnel integration and talent
    development, 149
phases, 8–12
principles, 12–14
repeatable processes, 150
resource sharing and benefit
    maximization, 150
responsibilities for managers, 14–18
stakeholder communication, 12–13
technological dimension, 140
vision, 12–13
IT-enabled Program Manager
agile adaptation management,
    18–19
ambidextrous management, 19–20
competencies for, 18–21
core functions of, 14–24
digital literacy, 21
downward alignment responsibility,
    16–17
dynamic stakeholder coordination,
    20–21
integrated conflict management, 19
interfacing connection
    responsibility, 17–18
responsibilities for, 14–18
upward alignment responsibility,
    15–16
IT project, 11, 17–20, 79, 118, 120
Iterative process, 7, 11

Key performance indicators (KPI)s,
    30, 32–33, 118

Learning program management, 21–24
applicability of knowledge and
    tools, 22
dynamic nature of work, 22
knowledge, 23–24

Manage change transition, 142
Measuring Benefits, 105–109
Monitoring benefit realization,
    112–115
Monitoring strategy, 93, 94

Net Present Value (NPV), 104

Objective management, 10–11
Operational benefits, 105
Operational management, 3
Organizational strategy, 115–117
Organizational Strategy Map, 41, 42
Organizational transformation, 2
Organizational Transformation
    Strategy, 35–36
Outcomes, 80

Performance metrics, 108, 133
Plan the change, 142
Planning pre-program
    Organizational Strategy Map, 41
    Program Vision Statement, 46–50
    Stakeholder Map, 41, 43–46
Program benefit goals, 117–120
Program benefits identifying,
    defining, and planning,
    77–78
Program benefits planning, 78
Program benefits realization,
    78, 110, 112
Program Blueprint, 13–14, 73, 145
    content, 77–78
    developing, 74–78
    digital integration, 76
    identifying, defining, and planning
        program benefits, 77–78
    purpose, 74–75
Program Brief, 58–62
    content, 61–62
    purpose, 60–61
    The Sun News, 58–60
Program Business Case
    contents, 73
    developing, 71–96
    planning process, 74
    purposes, 71–73
    relationship chart, 72
    review and approval, 96–97
Program Governance
    Arrangements, 73
    governance roles within program
        organization, 88, 92
Program Governance Board, 37–38

Program Governance Plan, 92–94
Program management, 3–7. *See also*
 IT-enabled management
 program
Program Management Maps, 73
Program Management Office
 (PMO), 95
Program Management Team, 38
 Program Manager, 39
 recruiting members, 39–40
Program Manager
 appointing, 39
 IT-enabled. *See* IT-enabled
  Program Manager
Program Mandate, 52–57, 145
 content, 56–57
 purpose, 52
 The Sun News, 54–56
Program Organizational Structure, 73
 Business Change Manager, 95–96
 Program Management Office, 95
 roles, 94–95
Program Preparation Plan, 62–66
 content, 62, 66
 purpose, 62
 The Sun News, 63–65
Program Sponsor, 35–36
Program Strategy Map, 145
 content, 51–52
 purpose, 51
 The Sun News, 53
Program Vision, 36, 46–50
Program Vision Statement, 46–50, 61
Project deliverables, 117–120
Project Dossier, 73, 146
 content, 87–88
 developing, 87
 purpose, 87
 reviewing and revising, 120–125
 The Sun News, 88–91, 121–124
Project output, 74, 77–80, 103

Quality and assurance management
 strategy, 93, 94

Realizing benefits, 104
Resource management strategy, 93, 94
Return on investment (ROI), 104

Risk management
 defining and planning IT-enabled
  program phase, 97–98
 executing and delivering
  IT-enabled program
  phase, 126–127
 identifying and formulating
  IT-enabled program
  phase, 67–68
 IT-enabled management
  program, 13
 strategy, 93, 94

Senior Responsible Owner (SRO), 37
Social engagement, 108
Social influence, 108–109
Sponsoring Group, 15–17, 36–37
 Program Governance Board, 37–38
 Senior Responsible Owner, 37
Stakeholder communication
  management
 aligning project design
  with program benefit
  objectives, 120
 program benefit goals with
  organizational strategy,
  115–117
 project deliverables with program
  benefit goals, 117–120
 reviewing and revising Project
  Dossier, 120–125
Stakeholder coordination,
  dynamic, 20–21
Stakeholder engagement strategy,
  93, 94
Stakeholder Map, 41
 high power, high interest, 43, 45
 high power, low interest, 45
 low power, high interest, 45–46
 low power, low interest, 46
Stakeholder Profile, 46, 47–48
Stakeholders, 43
 analysis, 10
 identifying and analyzing, 41,
  43–46
Strategic Alignment Model, 146
Strategic benefits, 105
Strategy execution, 3, 6

Strategy implementation, 3, 5, 7
  digital transformation, 147
  goal-driven, 149
The Sun News, 23–24, 26–33, 40
  Benefit Map, 84, 106
  Benefit Profile, 83
  benefit realization, 110, 112
  benefits achievement, 111,
     113–114
  digital integration Program
     Blueprint, 76
  Organizational Strategy Map, 42
  power and interest matrix, 49
  Program Brief, 58–60
  Program Mandate, 54–56
  Program Preparation Plan, 63–65
  Program Strategy Map, 53
  program vision, 49
  Project Dossier, 88–91, 121–124
  Stakeholder Map, 44
  Stakeholder Profile, 47–48
  state of, 75

Supporting project, 7
Sustain the change, 142
Sustaining benefits, 103–105
System integration phase, 147–148

Technology competitive potential
     phase, 148
Technology service phase, 148
Technology transformation phase, 148
Tracking benefit realization, 109–110

Uncertainty, 18, 115, 116, 126–127
Upward alignment responsibility,
     15–16

Video News Production
     Capability, 85
Vision Statement and a Program
     Brief, 10
Volatility, Uncertainty, Complexity,
     and Ambiguity (VUCA), 18,
     115, 116, 126–127

www.ingramcontent.com/pod-product-compliance
Lightning Source LLC
Chambersburg PA
CBHW061304220326
41599CB00026B/4727